Soccer–The 4-4-2 System

Soccer –
The 4-4-2 System

Thomas Dooley & Christian Titz

Meyer & Meyer Sport

Photo & Illustration Credits:

Cover Photos: imago, © fotolia/Rainer Claus
Cover Design: Sabine Groten
Illustrations: www.easy2coach.net

Translated from the original German by Matt Beadle (CETraining)

British Library Cataloguing in Publication Data
A catalogue record for this book is available from the British Library

Thomas Dooley & Christian Titz
Soccer – The 4-4-2 System
Maidenhead: Meyer & Meyer Sport (UK) Ltd., 2011
ISBN 978-1-84126-307-6

© 2011 by Meyer & Meyer Sport
Auckland, Beirut, Budapest, Cairo, Cape Town, Dubai, Graz, Indianapolis,
Maidenhead, Melbourne, Olten, Singapore, Tehran, Toronto
Member of the World
Sport Publishers' Association (WSPA)
www.w-s-p-a.org

Printed and bound by: B.O.S.S Druck und Medien GmbH, Germany
ISBN 978-1-84126-307-6
E-Mail: info@m-m-sports.com
www.m-m-sports.com

Table of contents

Foreword 7
1. **Criteria of tactical training** 8
2. **Variations of the system differentiations in 4-4-2** 9
   - General areas of play 9
   - Positional areas of play 10
   - 4-4-2 formation – Line formation/basic variations in the defence 12
   - 4-4-2 formation with the diamond as basic/defensive variant 13
   - 4-4-2 linear formation as 2-4-4 offensive variant 14
   - 4-4-2 formation with the diamond as offensive variant 15
3. **Positions in the 4-4-2 formation** 16
   - Goalkeeper 17
   - Wingback 18
   - Central defender 19
   - Outside midfielder 20
   - Central defensive midfielder/defensive halfback 21
   - Halfback midfielder 22
   - Central attacking midfielder 23
   - Center forward 24
   - Winger 25
   - Counterattacker 26
   - Striker in a two-man attack 27
4. **General and position-orientated tactical tasks in the 4-4-2 formation** 28
5. **Tactical setup of the 4-4-2 formation** 41
   - Engage – 2 defenders against an attacker 42
   - Engage 2 on 2 44
   - 2 on 2 – Engage with handover 46
   - 2 on 2 – Engage without handover 48
   - Back three – Basic organization 50
   - Back three – Shift to the left 52
   - Back three – Shift to the right 54
   - Back three – Forming triangles 56
   General/basic 4-4-2 formation with lettering of the positions 58
   - Back four – Basic formation 60
   - Back four – Shift to the left 62
   - Back four – Shift to the right 64
   - Back four – Shift to the right with fixed positioning in the center 66
   - Back four – Move to the right with engaging of the outer left midfielder 68
   - Back four – Left side central defender moving out 70
   - Back four – Right side central defender moving out 72
   - Back four – Left side central defender safeguarding after a deep pass 74
   - Back four – Right side central defender safeguarding after a deep pass 76
   - Back four – Right back safeguards after a deep pass .78
   - Back four – Left back safeguards after a deep pass 80
   - Zoning – Standing deep/dropping-pressing zone 82
   - Zoning – Defensive pressing 83
   - Zoning – Midfield pressing 84
   - Zoning – Attacking pressing 85
   - Basic formation 4-4-2 – Forming pairs 86
   - Right outer midfielder paths in 4-4-2 87
   - Forming triangles to safeguard 88

Table of contents

- Shadow covering 89
- Shifting together – Right central defender opens up play 90
- Shifting together – Possession with right center-back 92
- Shifting together – Possession with left back 94
- Shifting together – Ball zone inside left midfielder 96
- Shifting together – Ball zone inside right midfielder 98
- Shifting together – Ball zone between left back and left midfielder 100
- Shifting together – Ball zone between right back and right midfielder 102
- Shifting together – Ball played to the opposition's left striker 104
- Shifting together – Pass between the two rows of four 106
- Shifting together – Wingback is outplayed 108
- Shifting together – Wingback attacked 110
- Shifting together – Both lines of four are outplayed by a long line ball 112
- Shifting together to the right side central defender in attacking pressing 114
  Notes on pressing 116
- Channel the play inward in 4-4-2 linear formation 118
- Channel the play inward in 4-4-2 diamond formation 120

6. **Methodical set-up of the 4-4-2 formation or the back four** **122**
7. **Training unit 4-4-2** **123**
   Tactical movement in the 4-4-2 formation 123
   - Warming up in the 4-4-2 linear system 124
   - Warming up in the 4-4-2 linear system with balls 126
   - Warming up in the 4-4-2 diamond system with balls 128
   - Alternative warming up routine – Running in chains 130
   Main part I 133
   - One attacker against two defenders 134
   - Two against two with moving in 136
   - Two defenders against three attackers 138
   - Three defenders against five attackers 140
   Main part II 142
   - Type of play I – path of the back-four with 8 players 142
   - Type of play II – paths of the back four with 4 players + 1 144
   - Type of play III – 4 defenders against 7 attackers 146
   Main part III 150
   - 4 defenders + 1 central midfielder against 7 attackers 150
   End of Training 153
   - Another training example: 5 against 3 constantly in turns 154

Acknowledgements **156**

For access to exclusive Easy2Coach animations, see page 149

The 4-4-2-system is one of the most commonly used formations in modern football. The diamond, a flat four or positional marking, is a term that everyone connected to soccer is familiar with.

This book is dedicated to outlining the training connected with the 4-4-2-system. Using numerous, methodical training drill examples, this book presents the most important and effective training exercises required to learn the 4-4-2-system and successfully implement it into your everyday training schedule.

So what does methodical tactical training look like? How do I coach runs and movement? How does a team switch sides as a unit? How do I set-up zonal pressing and where does each player need to position him/herself?

We have attempted to answer all of these questions (and many more) through selected drills and phases of play. All the exercises in this book are the result of years of practical experience in amateur and professional soccer.

Each exercise contains detailed instructions, which should help you ensure correct implementation.

We hope that we have been successful in offering something for those interested in tactics and in particular specific, understandable, practical examples of measured tactical exercises related to the 4-4-2-system.

Enjoy the book and your coaching!

Christian Titz & Thomas Dooley

The strategic guide to a game includes:

- Finding the correct tactical solutions
- Game tactics
- Individual, group, and team tactics
- Tactics are not measured by means of testing

What are tactics?

a) The deployment of my resources considering tactical possibilities and basic conditions while taking into account the opposition's resources
b) Score goals, prevent goals

Features:

- Strategy is the idea, the tactics (the system) the implementation.
- Tactical orientation is coupled with fitness and technical proficiencies, as well as with the game intelligence, coordination and psychological characteristics of a team.
- The basic requirement for the implementation of a tactic is the team's willingness to learn new things. As a coach you are instrumental in laying the corresponding foundations through verbal and visual explanations. The team's willingness depends primarily on their trust in the coach's capabilities and his ways and means of assembling in training and matches.

Tactical learning/playing styles:

(a) Experience
(b) Theory – illustrating on a board, video analysis, discussions during and after the game/after training
(c) Training/Playing styles
(d) 'Freezing' a game situation on the field (everybody immediately stands still at the command of the coach)
(e) Players themselves watch games (learning, observing). Afterward the discussion about the match is important
(f) Incorporate mistakes from matches into training work (i.e., make use of the mistakes in training)

General areas of play

Implementation
The playing field can be subdivided into 4 playing zones. The following playing features should be observed in the respective zones

Goalscoring area - defense (endline-22m)
- Act safely
- No risky passes
- Opening up the game can be achieved by long line or diagonal passes
- Little dribbling, done carefully
- Short passing game should be flat
- Systematic and rigorous in challenges with the opposition

Midfield zone defensive
- Simple, short passing game
- Rather less dribbling
- Avoid high passes
- Passing with the back to the opposition has risks
- Emergence of offensive action owing to the opposition

Midfield zone offensive
- Accept risky plays
- Zone for setting up goals
- Passing zone during the opening up of play
- Good ball-winning zone when the opposition has possession
- Creative zone
- 1 on 1 situations

offensive danger zone

midfield offensive zone

defensive midfield zone

defensive danger zone

22m

Goalscoring area attack (endline-22m)
- Creative action zone
- Goalscoring area
- Good area for dead ball situations
- There is often a chance of scoring during won 1 on 1 situations and cases where the opposition is outnumbered
- Room for strikers and offensive midfielders

Positional areas of play

Implementation:
In the following zones (the width of the outer areas 15-20m – the width of the middle area approx. 15m – the length of the individual areas is identical) the players move about in the ball orientated zone-defense in defense as well as in the attacking game (dribbling to break down the opposition, 1 on 1 situations in goalscoring areas, counter-attacking the opponent or their own unorganized defense, as well as dead ball situations are all exempt from this).

Goalkeepers:
B+C, occasionally A+D, very rarely F+G

Left fullback:
Defensive zone – A, B, E, F, I, J
Attack zone – E, F, I, J, M

Right fullback:
Defensive zone – C, D, G, H, K, L
Attack zone – G, H, K, L, P

Right central defender:
Defensive zone – C, B, G, F more rarely D, H
Attack zone – G, F, K, J

Left central defender:
Defensive zone – B, C, F, G more rarely A, E
Attack zone – F, G, J, K

Right midfielder/Winger:
Defensive zone – G,H,K, L, more rarely C, D
Attack zone – K, L, O, P

Left midfielder/Winger:
Defensive zone – E, F, I, J, more rarely A, B
Attack zone – I, J, M, N

Central defensive midfielder:
Defensive zone – F, G, J, K, occasionally doubling up at B, C
Attack zone – F, G, J, K

Midfielder - right halfback:
Defensive zone – G, H, K, L more rarely J, F
Attack zone – G, J, K, O, more rarely P

Midfielder - left halfback:
Defensive zone – E, F, I, J, more rarely G, K
Attack zone – I, F, J, N, more rarely M

Attacking central midfielder:
Defensive zone – F, G, J, K, selten I, L
Attack zone – J, K, N, O, occasionally I, M, P, L

Right striker in a two-man attack/center forward/counter attacker:
Defensive zone – F, G, H, J, K, L
Attack zone – J, K, L, N, O, P

Left striker in a two-man attack/center forward/counter attacker:
Defensive zone – E, F, G, I, J, K
Attack zone – I, J, K, M, N, O

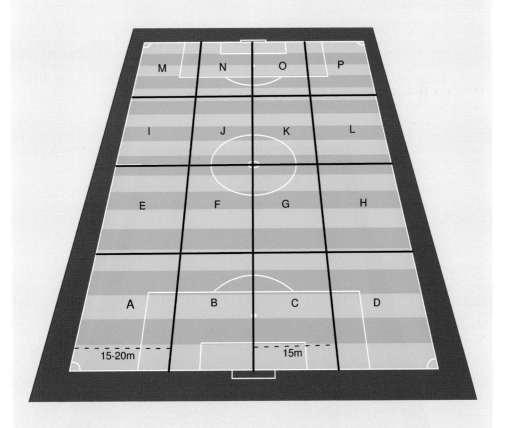

Training Target
- **Tactics**

Training Aspects

Training structure:	Main point/Emphasis
Participating players:	Whole team
Duration:	10-30 min

Organization:
Placement of ten outfield players and a goalkeeper on the playing field. The players will be positioned in 4 lines according to their positions (goalkeeper/defender/midfielder/strikeforce).

Implementation:
The 4-4-2 positioning corresponds to the basic formation in linear scaling. The first line is the goalkeeper. The second linear formation is the chain of four defenders, the third is the midfield chain and the fourth is the pair of strikers. When his own team has possession of the ball, the goalkeeper moves from his goal to the middle of his own half of the field, so that he has a distance of approximately 20 meters to his defense and can always play as somewhat of a sweeper. The individual chains of outfield players have a distance of 8-12 meters between themselves and the next chain, and between 7-12 meters distance in width between themselves and the next player beside him. In this system, two central defenders and two wingbacks are played in the row of defenders, the midfield is composed of two defensive midfielders playing in the half-back positions, two wide midfielders, and two strikers.

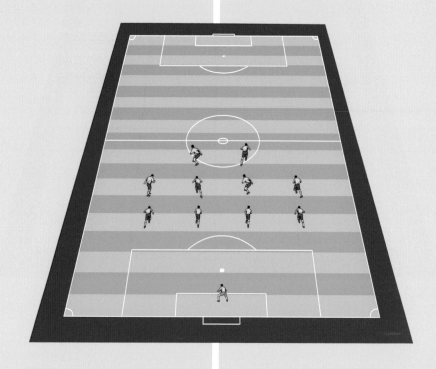

Training Target
- **Tactics**

Training Aspects

Training structure:	**Main point/Emphasis**
Participating players:	**Whole team**
Duration:	**10-30 min**

Organization:
The 4-4-2 formation is constructed as 4-4-2 in diamond formation in midfield. It involves the positioning of 10 outfield players and a goalkeeper on the playing field. The players are positioned according to their positions in four sections of position (goalkeeper/defense/midfield/strikeforce).

Implementation:
The 4-4-2 diamond formation conforms with the basic formation in the defensive and strikeforce scaling. However, in midfield, the formation is not operated "in line", but in the diamond formation from which the name comes, with one player in the defensive midfield position, two players in the half-back positions and one attacking midfielder behind the two strikers. The first line is the goalkeeper. The second line formation is the chain of four defenders, the third the midfield and the fourth the strike partnership. While his team has possession of the ball, the goalkeeper moves between his own goal and the middle of his own half of the pitch, so that there's a distance of approximately 20 meters between him and the defensive line, meaning he can also play as somewhat of a sweeper. Between the chains of players there is a distance of 8-12 meters in length and between 7-12 meters in width between them and the next player.

Training Target

- **Tactics**

Training Aspects

Training structure:	Main point/Emphasis
Participating players:	Whole team
Duration:	10-30 min

Organization:

The 4-4-2 formation is positioned as an offensive variant in a 2-4-4 formation. It involves the positioning of 10 outfield players and a goalkeeper on the playing field. The players are positioned according to their location in four lines (goalkeeper/defense/midfield/strikeforce).

Implementation:

The offensive formation arises out of the 4-4-2 linear scaling, where now the players take up an offensive position. The aim is to exploit the whole width and depth of the playing field in order to maintain a larger playing space for the formation of the team's attack. The first line is the goalkeeper. The second is the chain of four defenders. Here the central defenders stand 20-30 meters apart from each other. The wingbacks move to the touchline and can be shifted slightly upfield (how far depends on the opposition's tactics). They practically act as midfielders. In the third line, the chain of midfielders, the outside midfielders become wingers and the two central players in the halfback positions are moved back slightly as well as laterally towards each other, and serve as distributors of the ball. The fourth line is the strike partnership; one of the two takes up a deep position, the other an ever so slightly "second striker" position. While his team has possession of the ball, the goalkeeper moves between his own goal and the middle of his own half of the field so that there's a distance of approximately 20 meters between him and the defensive line and he can play as somewhat of a sweeper.

Training Target
- **Tactics**

Training Aspects

Training structure:	Main point/Emphasis
Participating players:	Whole team
Duration:	10-30 min

Organization:

The 4-4-2 formation is constructed as an offensive variant in a 2-4-4 diamond formation. It involves the positioning of 10 outfield players and a goalkeeper on the playing field. The players are positioned according to their positions in four lines (goalkeeper/defense/midfield/strikeforce).

Implementation:

This is a 4-4-2 linear scaling with a midfield diamond, where one player now takes up an attack position. The aim is to use the whole width and depth of the field in order to maintain a larger playing space for the formation of the team's attacking game. The first line is the goalkeeper. The second chain consists of four defenders. Here the central defenders stand 20-30 meters apart

from each other. The wingbacks move to the touchline and can be shifted slightly up field (how far depends on the opposition's tactics). They practically act as midfielders. In the third line the defensive midfielder is positioned deep as a safeguard and the central attacking midfielder drives on behind or occasionally in the strikeforce. The fourth line is the strike partnership; one of the two takes up a deep position, the other an ever so slightly "second striker" position. While his team has possession of the ball, the goalkeeper moves between his own goal and the middle of his own half of the field, so that there's a distance of approximately 20 meters between him and the defensive line and he can play as somewhat of a sweeper.

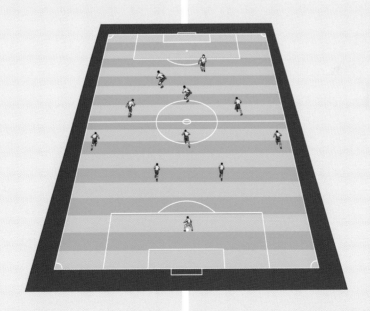

Training Target

- **Tactics**

Training Aspects

Participating players:

Whole team

The following positions and their individual tasks will be introduced on the following pages:

- Goalkeeper
- Wingback
- Central defender
- Outside midfielder
- Central defensive midfielder/defensive halfback
- Halfback midfielder
- Central attacking midfielder
- Center forward
- Winger
- Counterattacker
- Striker in a two-man attack

Goalkeeper

- Precise, direct passing game
- Tactical understanding and good anticipation of the game
- Coaching the rearguard
- Co-managing the game's pace or speed (quick switch from defense to attack, calming the game through keeping the ball, ball control, etc.)
- Distinctive hand-eye coordination, very good technical ball skills with feet and hands (dealing tidily with backpasses/passes, initiating attacks through neat and quick played flat and aerial balls, targeted free kicks, throwing out the ball or punting the ball in a drop-kick style)
- Good governing of the penalty area
- Good defensive skills on the line and in 1 on 1 situations
- Strong jumping strength and jumping dynamism coupled with superior coordination
- Strong psychological stability
- Physical requirements include being tall (should be above 6ft) and a large reach

Fundamentally the modern goalkeeper must have the capabilities of an outfield player at his command, complemented by his goalkeeper-specific skills. The goalkeeper acts as a type of sweeper who is always involved in the game, directs those in front of him, and deals with passes from the opposition.

Wingback

- Ball-winning ability
- The skills of a winger in attack (running down the flanks and quick dribbling)
- Above average speed and mobility (especially quickness off the mark)
- Co-managing the game's pace or speed (quick switch from defense to attack, calming the game through keeping possession of the ball, ball control, etc.)
- Precise, direct passing game. Very good long and diagonal passes (these are conducive to open build ups and switches in play)
- Tactical understanding and good anticipation of the game, specifically good positional play with the emphasis on doubling up, moving in, moving up, situationally forcing the opposition outwards or advancing outwards
- Plenty of willingness to run distances of 30 meters or more
- High level of understanding for the game especially concerning the switch of a defensive to offensive attitude and vice versa
- The courage to take risks
- Robustness

Fundamentally, the wingback must have the capabilities of a defensive player at his command, complemented by his attacking skills, which resemble those of a winger. He constantly moves between the defensive, midfield, and offensive zones and has a high workload involving long distance running to get the ball through.

Central defender

- Assured positional play
- High levels of basic speed
- Explosive acceleration
- High levels of dynamism coupled with good agility
- Good physical robustness and body size
- Good managing of the ball and a precise, powerful passing game
- Good vision of play and creative, situational build-up play
- Outstanding tackling abilities
- Excellent heading of the ball
- Very good tactical understanding (reciprocal safeguarding, setting in-depth, forming triangles, closing the area of the field close to the goal)
- Good anticipation and speed of action
- Quality in attacking play (switching to attacking play depending on the situation, dead ball situations)
- High concentration levels, resistant to pressure and good risk assessment
- Leadership qualities, organizer of the defense and transmitter of commands (offside)
- Precise short and long passing game, as well as diagonal volleyballs made with the side of the foot

Outside midfielder

- Great acceleration and pace over a distance, agility, dynamism and good stamina
- More of a smaller, strong dribbling, tricky player with a hunger for goals
- Systematic switch from attack to defense and vice versa
- Having lost the possession of the ball, goes on an immediate, aggressive pursuit to regain the ball
- Willingness to take risks to sprint to the flanks or attempt to succeed in a 1 on 1 situation
- Good execution of dead ball situations (corner kicks, mid-range free kicks, etc.)
- Assured in combinations
- Physical robustness
- Good positional play, especially when moving in
- Good understanding of the game
- Ability to suddenly stop (cut back) and change direction while dribbling quickly

This type of player is like a winger who possesses the defensive qualities of a defensive midfielder. He is always moving between the midfield and attacking zones and, as a result, has a high workload involving long distance running.

Central defensive midfielder/defensive halfback

- Outstanding tactical behavior during build-up play
- Ability to develop strategies to win the ball when the opposition has possession or to demand the corresponding patterns
- Very good vision of play
- Accomplished in dribbling
- Enormously safe short passing game
- Quick, systematic switch from attack to defense and vice versa
- Very strong ball-winning abilities in attacking as well as defensive challenges (stronger emphasis of quality on the defensive tackles)
- Very good ability to read play and to quickly react (shaping the game's pace, switching from attack to defense). A very strong ability to anticipate results in well-organized pressing play
- Leading player with high levels of acceptance and responsibility in the team
- A willingness to run and be a team leader. Decisive with a balanced mixture of being dominant and behaving as a team player should
- Above-average technical play and pace
- Safety on the ball and when passing
- Good heading game and a hard and precise shot from distance

Halfback midfielder

- Outstanding tactical behavior during build-up play
- Ability to develop strategies to win the ball when the opposition has possession or to be able to demand the corresponding patterns
- Very good vision of play
- Quick dribbling and mastery of extensive repertoire of maneuvers
- Strong in offensive 1 on 1 situations
- Quick, systematic switch from attack to defense and vice versa
- Strong in defense
- Through his important position in the build-up of play, he can vary the speed of play and read the game very well
- Good ability to react quickly
- A large willingness to run
- Above-average technical play and pace
- Safety on the ball and when passing
- Has a good shot on goal and is generally dangerous in front of goal

Fundamentally, a player in this position can be a central defensive midfielder, winger or a central anchorman. His role depends on the playing philosophy of the coach. He combines the abilities of an offensive and defensive player. He moves between the defensive, midfield, and attack zones and therefore has a high workload of running.

Central attacking midfielder

- Good anticipation of play/understanding of game situations
- Good management of the ball and a precise, powerful passing game
- Good vision of play and a creative, situational build-up play
- Good demeanor in offensive duels
- High playing intelligence and creativity
- Distributor of ideas and passes
- Acts quickly
- Good strength of shots and dangerous in dead ball situations (penalties, free kick attempts on goal, etc.)
- Good ball control, good on the ball and keeping possession
- Quick acceleration
- Outstanding technical play and vision of the game
- Quick, lively movements coupled with the ability to make split-second decisions, whether it be by starting a 1 on 1 situation where the opposition is overpowered, starting a paced dribble or playing a deep ball
- Reads the quality of a player's abilities and consequently decides with which players a quick short pass is possible
- Great timing in passing and the ability to start running
- Has indispensable qualities for the team in the attacking areas, which can win matches

Center forward

- Robust type of player who is a strong header of the ball and who hovers in the air with great timing when jumping
- Good vision of play
- Shields the ball well and can consequently deploy players coming up in support
- Has enormous technical abilities while under the highest pressure (ball control, dribbling, passing game, keeping possession of the ball)
- Agile in the penalty box
- Type of player who can jump well and accelerate quickly
- In addition to his ability to strike the ball well with both feet, he also has at his disposal an eye for the goal
- Has the talent to read the play and anticipate and recognize goalscoring opportunities
- Stands out due to his readiness for action and to battle

Winger

- Great hunger for goals and great goal-scoring instincts
- Swift as an arrow
- Good safety on the ball
- Clever and shrewd with plays
- Good ability to assert himself and get things done coupled with an extensive repertoire of maneuvers
- One of the first defenders in the defensive network
- Has a very good shooting technique at his disposal, particularly in volleying the ball
- Excellent in executing quick counterattacks
- Good crosser and executor of dead ball plays (corners, mid-range free kicks, etc.)
- Good anticipation
- Very good at timing his take-offs, when he has to make runs into free space or to intercept the ball
- Good at receiving the ball and moving on (stop and go)
- Works with the ball at a high pace without losing speed
- Quick off the mark with tremendous acceleration
- Rapid dribbling with the ability to utilize tricks and dummies at the same time
- Quicker, livelier type of player who, at the highest pace, can perform changes in direction with the ball at his feet
- Moves with his running motion, often on the balls of his feet

Counterattacker

- Great hunger for goals and goal-scoring instincts
- Swift as an arrow
- Good safety on the ball
- Clever and shrewd in play
- Good ability to assert himself, which is peppered with an extensive repertoire of maneuvers
- Has a very good shooting technique, particularly in volleying the ball
- Very good at timing his take-offs, when he has to make runs into free space/interface
- Good at receiving the ball and moving on (stop and go) at the highest pace without losing any speed in the process
- Is explosive off the mark with tremendous acceleration while the ball is at his feet. Also has the ability to execute maneuvers at the same time
- Quicker, livelier type of player who at the highest speed can perform changes in direction with the ball at his feet
- Moves with a good running style often on the balls of his feet
- Good dribbling that spans over space with close ball control

Striker in a two-man attack

- Good acceleration, quick speed of action
- Neat ball control
- With his back to the opponent, he works very well with the ball and can consequently deploy players coming up in support
- Ability to sense goalscoring opportunities
- Dangerous in front of goal, is a quality finisher and has nerves of steel
- Can unlock a 1 on 1 situation and has a repertoire of tricks
- Has good dribbling skills in tight spaces, and is able to quickly dribble over space at speed
- Good assertiveness

Both players in the strikeforce can be the same type of player, or a combination of an attacking midfielder, winger, center forward or counter attacker can also be used.

General and position-orientated tactical tasks in the 4-4-2 formation

The 4-4-2 formation defines the number of players in the individual parts of the team. The goalkeeper is excluded from this. In this formation, with four defensive players, four midfielders and two strikers, the coach is given more variations to adapt, which in each case can be distinguished from each other by the positioning of the midfielders.

Tactically much more can be involved than merely sending the players onto the field in a certain formation. It is the coach's (and club's) philosophy of how to play and the available qualities of the players that are the deciding factors that determine how a formation will ultimately be tactically implemented on the playing field.

The 4-4-2 formation thereby represents one of a number of possibilities.
Through the different ways and means of positioning players on the pitch, six to seven sections with many triangle formations and play-to points emerge for each offensive structure. In the defensive unit, three to four sections are formed depending on the chosen defensive formation.

The two most common variations of the 4-4-2 formation are the 4-4-2 diamond formation and the 4-4-2 linear formation with a so-called "flat four". Both of these will now be introduced with their most important characteristics. The focus will be on the most commonly used formation with the flat four.

4-4-2 with a midfield diamond
In the diamond formation, a chain of four defenders, a defensive central midfielder, two players in the halfback positions, an attacking central anchorman midfielder and two strikers are played. The main focus is put on attacking play through the middle.

4-4-2 with flat four
In this system, there is no anchorman behind the strikers. The subdivision of the four available midfielders takes place with two defensively oriented players in the halfback positions and two offensively oriented players on the flanks. The positioning of the set of defenders and strikers conforms to that which was described in the diamond formation. The main focus is put on closing the space in front of the team's own defense.

Advantages of the 4-4-2 with a midfield diamond
- Creative attacking play through central, offensive midfielders
- The emergence of a situation in attack where the opposition's defense is outnumbered
- Strengthened attacking play through the middle
- Strengthened integration with the strikers
- Increased passing possibilities through the formation of triangles between players

Moving the left back and right back farther up the field when in possession of the ball and positioning the two strikers staggered in a deep lying position establishes seven (playing) sections in the attacking play with a triangular positioning of the players. This leads to a higher number of passing options.

Disadvantages of the 4-4-2 with a midfield diamond

- Susceptibility to quick counter attacks through the middle (only one defensively orientated central midfielder).

- Free space on the flanks in the area between the wingback and the midfielders in the half-back position.

- Increased susceptibility to attacking plays down the wings, as the wingbacks in this formation must be attack oriented.

Advantages of the 4-4-2 with flat four

- Concentrated safeguarding in the center of midfield courtesy of the two central defensive midfielders.

- Strengthened play down the flanks when in possession of the ball through the offensive orientation of the two wide midfielders.

- The flanks are occupied without the wingbacks having to move completely forward (defensive cover guaranteed). The flanks are doubly occupied so outnumbering the opposition can be accomplished easier or crosses can be played.

- Owing to greater open space between the attack and the center of midfield, the strikers can be played in these open areas and consequently a defender can be drawn out of the defense, or the wide midfielders have the opportunity here to cut inside by dribbling the ball.

Disadvantages of the 4-4-2 with flat four

- Due to the offensive orientation of the two wide midfielders, free space/situations where the team is outnumbered by the opposition come about through quick counterattacks by the opposition.

- There is no central attacking midfielder, and therefore also no additional, creative player who can play passes from the middle into the deeper positions or who can storm into the middle with a dribble. As a result, the opportunity to create direct shots on goal from such plays is lost, along with the opportunity to create open space for the attackers and wide midfielders.

- Large areas of open space in the area between the attack and central midfield.

- In the attacking formation, there are fewer different sections of play as a result of the two attacking wingbacks and staggered strikers than in the diamond formation. Hence only six points to play exists versus the diamond formation.

The 4-4-2 system with flat four in detailed information (with comments on the diamond)

Defensive formation:
When the opposition has possession of the ball the team in the defensive unit should form the 4-4-2 linear formation in a maximum area of 35 x 35 meters. The defensive formation distinguishes its basic positioning via a linear positioning of the separate parts of the team. This means both the four defenders as well as the four midfielders and two strikers are positioned at a certain level. They therefore form 3 defensive lines. At the same time it is necessary for them to maintain a certain distance from each other, which guarantees an optimal defense of the team's goal. This distance as a general rule is as follows: 7-12 meters across and 8-15 meters in depth. The distance between the individual players and parts of the team can vary as a result of an erratic playing speed, change in the playing conditions or when the team's full complement of players is temporarily reduced.

When the opposition has possession of the ball, the defensive unit in the 4-4-2 diamond formation should likewise move in an area that is restricted to a maximum of 35 x 35 meters. The defensive formation is positioned as follows: The four defenders are positioned on one level, the central defensive midfielder, the midfielders in the halfback positions as well as the central attack are staggered in their positioning, and the two strikers are positioned on one level. Hence they form five lines of defense. One option is to move the midfielders in the halfback positions in line with the central defensive midfielder to form a line of three. This would then create only four lines of defense.

In the team's grouping, a compact, disciplined linear shift is intended, which aims to constrict space and consequently deny the opposition the possibility of playing passes into deep positions, and also prevent them from embarking on solo attempts. Directing the ball-carrying player towards the flanks and getting possession of the ball by pressing is all part of the most important tactical methods in the duel with the opposition, as is directing the opening up of play by the opposition team towards the players positioned out wide by use of the corresponding linear shift, and to block the way to pass so that only a pass to the middle is possible. There, the player will be doubled-up on and put under enormous pressure.

Defensive triangles and defensive shadowing
In the 4-4-2 formation, the diamond or line can be shifted. In play, triangles towards the ball, known as defensive triangles, are always being formed in an attempt to create a "defensive shadow." The defensive shadow is the space through which the opponent cannot pass or dribble owing to the triangular-shaped positioning of the players.

Zonal defense
A typical feature of the 4-4-2 system is the zonal defense. In the zonal defense, every player is assigned an area/zone for which he is responsible when the opposition has possession of the ball. When the opponent moves out of the zone, out of the player's "area of responsibility," he automatically enters the next player's zone and is "assumed" by him. The "delivering" player either stays in his area or assists his teammate in helping to defend his area by pressing the attacker. This decision depends predominantly on whether another attacker is moving in the delivering player's zone or not. Exception: In the area where one has a great chance on goal (16-22 meters from the team's goal), the opposition player is no longer passed over, as the handover of a player can cause a short moment of there being no cover, which a good player can use to score a goal.

Attack formation
The attack formation differs from the defensive position in the positioning of the wide players, in the positioning of the midfielders in the two halfback positions and of course in its fundamental game specific task/function.

Positioning of the central defenders
Both central defenders are positioned 20-30 meters across from each other in order to lend themselves as support players.

Positioning and tasks of the left back and right back
Both players move, depending on the situation in play, to approximately 10m in front of the halfway line going forward and up to the sideline going outwards. Both players actively participate in attack play, in which they, depending on the situation in play, "overlap", break

through to the baseline and cross, put in a mid-range cross or dribble diagonally towards the penalty area and hunt for the finish.

Positioning of the left and right midfielders
Both players move, depending on the situation in play, to the sideline and about 10m behind the halfway line. Both players support important attack endeavors and can interact with the advancing wingbacks, the striker on his side of the field or the midfielders.

Positioning of midfielders in the halfback positions
One of the two players joins attack plays in which he marches forward out of the linear formation and takes a significant part in the playing style. Shifts in play with diagonal passes to the players on the flanks, the playing of passes to strikers in deep positions, as well as calming the play by keeping hold of the ball and having a safe passing game are among his tasks. Generally, through his game, he significantly dictates the speed of the match.

Positioning of the strikers
One striker lies deeper and the other hangs back or hustles into any free spaces between the defensive and midfield chains. When the opponent lies deep, a situation also emerges where both strikers can be positioned on the same level. They regularly switch positions.

Task/function
The change in positioning, which fundamentally alters orientation of the team, is geared first and foremost towards creating chances on goal. In attack play, the game, in contrast to the compact defensive scaling, is arranged deeply and widely in order to gain as much room as possible for attack moves. A creative passing game and a willingness to take risks when dribbling with the ball and in the passing game replaces the defensive mentality of avoiding conceding goals.

Pressing zones
In soccer there are three pressing zones. The pressing zones describe the space in which the opposition team is attacked.

Defensive pressing zone
The area between the semicircle of the penalty area and the semicircle in front of the halfway line, or respectively 5-10m in front of the halfway line.

Midfield pressing zone
The area between the semicircle in front of the halfway line and the semicircle behind the halfway line, or respectively in each case up to 5m in front or behind that.

Attack pressing zone:
The area between the halfway line and the opponent's penalty box's semicircle, or respectively 4-5m in front of that.

In attack play, the strikers have a particular importance. Against a rearguard that is likewise playing in a chain formation, it is necessary to move shrewdly. If the strikers stand close, side by side, the wingbacks cannot move in, as in doing so they would leave the flanks open. Consequently, the wingbacks have the choice of either moving in and providing protection (flanks open) or covering the areas on the flanks and thus maintaining the chains in the linear formation which causes areas to emerge for passing at the point where players meet (in behind) in the back four.

Position-orientated tasks in the 4-4-2

Goalkeeper
- When his team has possession of the ball, he should march up no farther than the end of his own half of the pitch as someone his team can play to
- Acts as a sweeper
- Shifts left and right along the breadth of the goal inside the penalty area
- Must position himself deep enough to be playable to his central defenders and wing-backs
- Organizes his team in dead ball situations and helps the team to prevent tactical mistakes by arranging them and giving them instructions, or helps to correct any mistakes or errors
- Opens up play by throwing the ball out, taking goal kicks, punting the ball out his hands or passing in open play
- When the opposing team in possession of the ball is 30-35 meters from his goal, his alertness and tactical awareness should activate. The following range of examples highlights the diverse requirements of a goalkeeper: observes the opponent players' runs (especially the strikers'); observes and anticipates the ball as well as the ball's trajectory; when able, snuffs out 1 on 1 situations; intercepts crosses/free kicks and corner balls; builds walls in free kick situations; gives tactical directions to his teammates, motivates his team; and closes the angle for shots with correct positional play

A – left back
Defensive duties
- Supports the outer left midfielder
- Covers the touchline and prevents long line passes
- Moves in to the right when the left side central defender (B) moves forward to challenge the ball-carrying player
- Shifts backwards and to the right when the ball is transferred to the opposite side
- As the situation dictates the left back has to function as the left side central defender, once he has been outplayed and the actual central defender attacks the opponent, as otherwise the left back would arrive too late. He does not take up this position if, after having lost in the challenge, he can apprehend his opponent in time or the right midfielder moves into the back four. Then he can press with the left side central defender and help him in dealing with the attacking player
- His defensive path infield is, as a rule, up to the front post, unless the opposition player storms into a goal-scoring area, in which case he stays with him

Attack duties
- When in possession, he goes wide and deep in order to make the playing field larger
- Serves as a go-to point when his team has possession

- Moves in countermovements and offers himself as a go-to point for the midfielders and left side central defender
- Must agree with the left midfielder on when they want to switch positions or when he would like to overlap him
- Tries to dribble and put crosses in
- Has to calculate diagonal and through balls, and himself have a good short and long passing game

B – left side central defender
Defensive duties
- Moves backwards to the left and safeguards the left back when the left back attacks the opponent on the touchline
- Moves backwards to the right and safeguards the right side central defender in a triangular formation when the ball carrier attacks and shifts to the right or moves in if the ball is transferred to the right side of the defense in the direction of the touchline
- If a pass is played between the two defending defensive and midfield lines in a space with an opponent, the defender must gauge whether he should attack the player, position himself deeper or stay in his position
- He must always consider whether to sit deep or attack the opposition player
- Won't surrender in goal-scoring areas

Offensive duties
- Goes wide when in possession
- Organizes play with a quick short passing game to the wingbacks, the central midfielders or midfielders in the halfback position, or by long passes with the side of his foot into deep positions to the strikers or by diagonal passes to the flanks
- After attempting a pass out wide, he always maintains a certain depth so that he is free
- Shouldn't collide with the midfield line or the wingbacks
- Organizes the whole of the team's path in attacking and defensive play
- Joins in dead ball situations up front

C – right side central defender
Defensive duties
- Moves backwards to the right and safeguards the right back when the right back attacks the opponent on the touchline
- Moves backwards to the left and safeguards the left side central defender in a triangular formation when the ball carrier attacks and shifts to the right or moves in if the ball is transferred to the left side of the defense in the direction of the touchline
- If a pass is played between the two defending defensive and midfield lines in a space with an opponent, the defender must gauge whether he should attack the player, position himself deeper or stay in his position
- He must always consider whether to sit deep or attack the opposition player
- Won't surrender in goal-scoring areas

Offensive duties

- Goes wide when in possession
- Organizes play with a quick short passing game to the wing-backs, the central midfielders or midfielders in the halfback position, or by long passes with the side of his foot into deep positions to the strikers or by diagonal passes to the flanks
- After attempting a pass out wide, he always maintains a certain depth so that he is playable
- A high-speed dribble through the middle should be carefully considered because a loss of possession presents a good goal-scoring opportunity for the opposition
- Shouldn't collide with the midfield line or the wingbacks
- Organizes the whole of the team's path in attacking and defensive play
- Joins in dead ball situations up front
- Organizes where the players should stand and, how to build a wall when free kicks and corners are taken

D – right back

Defensive duties

- Supports the right midfielder
- Covers the touchline and prevents long line passes
- Moves in to the left when the right side central defender (B) moves forward to challenge the ball carrying player
- Shifts backwards and to the left when the ball is transferred to the opposite side
- As situation dictates, the right back has to function as the right side central defender, once he has been outplayed and the actual central defender attacks the opponent, as otherwise the right back would arrive too late. He does not take up this position if, after having lost in the challenge, he can apprehend his opponent in time or the left midfielder moves into the back four. In this situation, he can press with the right side central defender and help him in dealing with the attacking player
- His defensive path infield is, as a rule, up to the front post, unless the opposition player storms into a goal-scoring area, in which case he stays with him

Attack duties

- When in possession he goes wide and deep in order to make the playing field larger
- Serves as a go-to point when his team has possession
- Moves in countermovements and offers himself as a go-to point for the midfielders and right side central defender
- Must agree with the right midfielder on when they want to switch positions or when he would like to overlap him
- Tries to dribble and put crosses in
- Has to calculate diagonal and through balls, and have a good short and long passing game

E – left midfielder/winger

Defensive duties

- Supports the left back (A)
- Attacks the opposition right back alone or with the striker (I)
- Moves in to the right when the left striker (I) or the inside left midfielder (F) moves forward to attack the ball carrying player
- Must move in as the left back when the right back has been outplayed and the left back moves to the left side central defender position
- His defensive path inwards is, as a rule, up to the front post, unless the opposition player storms into a goal-scoring area, in which case he stays with him

Attack duties

- Moves deep and wide when in possession of the ball in order to make the playing field bigger
- Serves as a go-to point when his team has possession
- Moves in countermovements and offers himself as a go-to point for the midfielders, left sided central defender and left back as well as the left striker
- Has to make sure he's not standing in an offside position
- Attempts to cross the ball and dribble
- Changes positions with the striker at times
- Has to calculate diagonal and through balls

F – inside left midfielder

Defensive duties

- Supports the striker (I) in the path moving forwards, when the ball carrier runs in his zone
- Supports the central left defender (B) in the path moving backwards, when the ball is played to the opponent's right striker
- Moves behind to the left and safeguards the left midfielder (E), when (E) attacks his opponent on the flanks
- Moves behind to the right and safeguards the inside right midfielder (G) in a triangular formation, when (G) attacks the ball carrier and shuffles to the right or moves in when the ball is transferred to the righthand side of the defense in the direction of the touchline
- When a pass is played between the defending back four and the midfield where there happens to be opponent players, (F) moves into a deep position so that he has the opponent in front of him and can attack the player receiving the ball

Offensive duties

- Goes wide when the central defender has possession of the ball
- Offers himself in the center or inside left position as the go-to point for the central left defender and left back
- Attempts to shape the game through a quick short passing game, deep lying passes or diagonal balls
- Has to sometimes control the ball with his back to the opposition and utilize high-speed dribbling

- Organizes the paths of the team in attack and defensive play
- Good executor of dead ball situations

G – inside right midfielder
Defensive duties
- Supports the striker (J) in the path moving forward, when the ball carrier runs into his zone
- Supports the central right defender (C) in the path moving backwards when the ball is played to the opponent right striker
- Moves behind to the right and safeguards the right midfielder (H), when (H) attacks his opponent on the flanks
- Moves behind to the left and safeguards the inside left midfielder (F) in a triangular formation when F attacks the ball carrier and shuffles to the right or moves in when the ball is transferred to the righthand side of the defense in the direction of the touchline
- When a pass is played between the defending back four and the midfield where there happens to be opponent players, (G) moves into a deep position so that he has the opponent in front of him and can attack the player receiving the ball

Offensive duties
- Goes wide when the central defender has possession of the ball
- Offers himself in the center or inside right position as the go-to point for the central right defender and right back
- Attempts to shape the game through a quick, short passing game, deep lying passes or diagonal balls
- Has to sometimes control the ball with his back to the opposition and utilize high-speed dribbling
- Organizes the paths of the team in attacking and defensive play
- Good executor of dead ball situations

Central attacking midfielder
Defensive duties
- Supports the left and right striker in the path moving forward when the ball carrier runs into his zone
- Shifts to the left when the ball comes to the right back, and closes the space between the inside left midfielder and the left striker
- Shifts to the right when the ball comes to the left back, and closes the space between the inside right midfielder and the right striker
- Supports the two midfielders in the halfback position

Attack duties
- Goes to the middle or deep when the central defender/wingbacks/midfielders have possession of the ball
- Attempts to shape the game through a quick, short passing game or deep lying passes
- Has to sometimes control the ball with his back to the opposition and utilize high-speed dribbling or a short dribble to overcome his opponents
- Sets the stage for his team's strikers with a good passing game

- Often plays one-twos
- Good executor of dead ball situations

Central defensive midfielder
Defensive duties
- Supports the left and right central defenders, when the ball carrier runs into their zones or a pass goes there
- Shifts to the left when the ball comes to the left wingback/midfielder and safeguards him
- Shifts to the right when the ball comes to the right wingback/midfielder and safeguards him
- Supports the two midfielders in the halfback positions
- When a pass is played between the defending back four and the midfield where there are opponents, (G) moves into a deep position so that he has the opponent in front of him and can attack the player receiving the ball

Attack duties
- Moves to the middle when the central defenders/wingbacks/other midfielders have possession of the ball
- Attempts to shape the game through a quick, short passing game, diagonal balls or deep lying passes
- Has to sometimes control the ball with his back to the opposition and utilize high-speed dribbling or a short dribble to overcome his opponents
- Often plays one-twos
- Organizes the defensive performance
- Good executor of dead ball situations

H – right midfielder/winger
Defensive duties
- Supports the right back (D)
- Attacks the opposition left back alone or with the striker (J)
- Moves in to the left when the right striker (J) or the inside right midfielder (G) move forward to attack the ball-carrying player
- Must move in as the right back when the left back has been outplayed and the right back moves to the right side central defender position
- His defensive path inward is as a rule up to the first post, unless the opposition player storms into a goal-scoring area, in which case he stays with him

Attack duties
- Moves deep and wide when in possession of the ball in order to make the playing field bigger
- Serves as a go-to point when his team has possession
- Moves in countermovements and offers himself as a go-to point for the midfielders, right side central defender and right back, as well as the right striker
- Has to make sure he's not standing in an offside position

- Has to agree on changes in position with the right back and clarify who moves inwards and when, to ensure that A overlaps
- Attempts to cross the ball and dribble
- Changes positions with the striker at times
- Has to calculate diagonal and through balls

I – the left striker in the two-man strike partnership/counter striker/center forward
Defensive duties
- With the left midfielder (E) he presses the opponent's right back
- Presses the inside left midfielder (F) head-on
- Attacks the right side central defender
- Safeguards behind the striker (J), if he runs at the left side central defender
- Remains the most deeply staggered player if the striker (J) in pressing runs at the inside right midfielder
- Ensures the back area/the path for passing back to the opposition's left-side central defender, when the striker (J) runs at the left back
- When pressing with the purpose of channeling the opposition's game inwards he attacks the right sided central defender in such a way that he is cajoled into playing a pass out to the right or into the middle, or he blocks the right back and consequently opens up the middle
- When the right striker channels the play out, he drops into a position of fifth midfielder and along with the inner right midfielder, presses the player expecting the ball in the middle

Attack duties:
- When in possession of the ball, he goes deeper in order to make the playing field bigger
- Serves as a go-to point when his team has possession
- Moves in countermovements and intersects with his strike partner
- Has to make sure he's not standing in an offside position or moves into an offside position
- Has to agree with his strike partner as to who will go short or long, what distance they should be from one another, etc.
- Volunteers himself for deep played passes or high passes with his back to the opposition
- Moves in the open areas between the defensive and midfield lines

J – the right striker in the two-man attack/counter striker/center forward
Defensive duties
- With the right midfielder (H) he presses the opponent's left back
- Presses the inside left midfielder (F) head-on
- Attacks the left side central defender
- Safeguards behind the striker (I), if he runs at the right side central defender
- Remains the most deeply staggered player if the striker (I) is pressing, runs at the inside left midfielder

- Ensures the back area path for passing back to the opposition's right side central defender, when the striker (l) runs at the right back
- When pressing with the purpose of channeling the opposition's game inward, he attacks the left side central defender in such a way that he is forced into playing a pass out to the left or into the middle, or he blocks the right back and consequently opens up the middle
- When the left striker channels the play outward, he drops into a position of fifth midfielder and along with the inner left midfielder presses the player expecting the ball in the middle

Attack duties
- When in possession of the ball, he goes deeper in order to make the playing field bigger
- Serves as a go-to point when his team has possession
- Moves in countermovements and intersects with his strike partner
- Has to make sure he's not standing in an offside position or moves into an offside position
- Has to agree with his strike partner as to who will go short or long, what distance they should be from one another, etc.
- Volunteers himself for deep played passes or high passes with his back to the opposition
- Moves in the open areas between the defensive and midfield lines

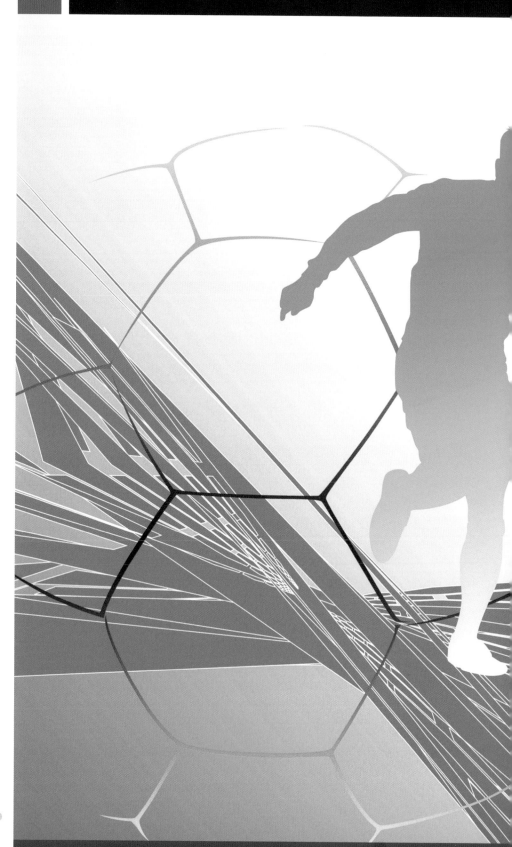

Tactical setup of the 4-4-2 formation

Training Target
- **Tactics**

Training Emphasis
- **Four man backfield**

Training Aspects

Skills involved:	Defensive play, Quick anticipation, Control, Dribbling, Quick decisions, Quick processing, Combining technical skill with movement, Body fake, Pushing
Age level:	13-14 years, 15 years to Adult, Under 12, Under 13
Level of play:	Beginner
Type of training:	Group training
Training structure:	Progression, Main point/Emphasis
Purpose:	Defensive behaviors, Improve individual qualities
Total number of players:	4 or more players
Participating players:	Whole team
Training location:	Any
Dealing with space:	Half field
Duration:	10-15 min
Physiology:	Soccer-specific endurance, Power & Speed
Goalkeeping:	1 goalie

Organization:
A goalkeeper and three outfield players position themselves on the field according to the diagram. The two blue players act as defenders, the red player as an attacker. The attacker has the ball.

Completing the drill:
The ball carrying attacker runs towards defender B. In doing so, he dribbles, alternating between feinting to the left and to the right. Player A safeguards player B by also matching C's lateral changes in direction.

If player B is outplayed, defender A immediately attacks player C while B safeguards player A from behind as quickly as possible and on his part follows player A's lateral changes in direction

Equipment:
One goal

Tips:
- At the start, the striker should only run at a moderate pace towards the defenders in order to give them the greatest chance possible to synchronize their runs.
- The distance of the rearmost defender to the one in front should always be approximately 5 meters.
- If the first defender has been passed, the rearmost defender runs to the attacker. When he's about 2-3 meters in front of him, he slows his speed, comes to a halt and running off-center backwards absorbs the attacker's speed.

Field size:
30 x 40 m

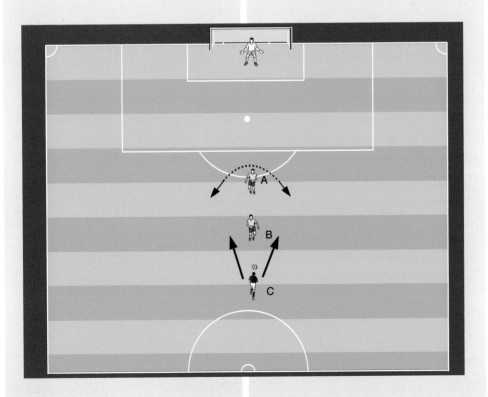

Training Target
- Tactics

Training Emphasis
- Four man backfield

Training Aspects

Skills involved:	Defensive play, Quick anticipation, Control, Quick decisions, Combining technical skill with movement, Short passing, Pushing
Age level:	13-14 years, Under 12, Under 13
Level of play:	Beginner
Type of training:	Group training
Training structure:	Progression, Main point/Emphasis
Purpose:	Defensive behaviors, Improve individual qualities
Total number of players:	4 or more players
Participating players:	Whole team
Training location:	Any
Dealing with space:	Half field
Duration:	10-15 min
Physiology:	Soccer-specific endurance, Power & Speed

Organization:
Four players position themselves on the field according to the diagram. The two blue players A and B act as defenders, the two red players are the attackers. The ball's starting position is with the red player C.

Completing the drill:
Player C starts with a pass to D. As soon as C moves to pass the ball, defender B comes running to/attacks player D. When leaving his defensive position in the direction of D, the defensive position of player B is taken over by player A. Then the players go back into their starting positions. The players to whom the ball is played change in a counterclockwise direction after each pass (so D to C, then B to C, etc.).

Equipment:
One goal

Tips:
- This exercise is a dry run. No tackling takes place. The primary function of the exercise is the learning of a basic soccer play.
- The exercise should be trained as many times as possible (to ensure automatic movement sequences).
- A precise and powerful passing game should be paid attention to.
- The start signal for the counter attack is when the passer of the ball moves to pass. The lateral distance between the players should consist of approximately 7-12m. The playing pairs stand approximately 15m opposite each other.

Field size:
15 x 15 m

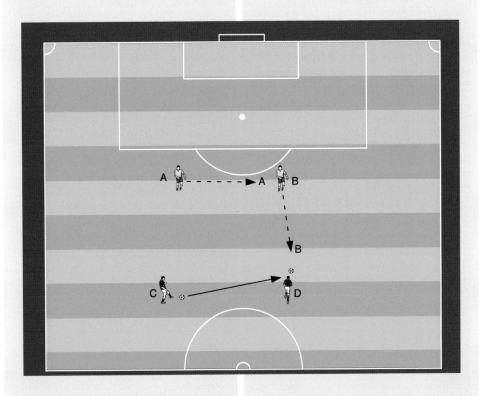

Training Target
- **Tactics**

Training Emphasis
- **Four man backfield**

Training Aspects

Skills involved:	Defensive/Offensive play, Quick anticipation, Controlling the ball, Dribbling, Quick decisions, Overlapping, Combining technical skill with movement, Short passing, Pushing
Age level:	13-14 years, 15 years to Adult, Under 11, Under 12
Level of play:	Beginner
Type of training:	Group training
Training structure:	Progression, Main point/Emphasis
Purpose:	Defensive behaviors, Offensive behaviors, Improve individual qualities
Total number of players:	4 or more players
Participating players:	Whole team
Training location:	Any
Dealing with space:	Half field
Duration:	10-15 min
Physiology:	Soccer-specific endurance

Organization:
Four players (blue A and B defenders/ red C and D attackers) are positioned on the field according to the diagram. The ball is with player C

Completing the drill:
The exercise starts with a pass from player C to player D, who immediately starts to dribble forward. Simultaneously, player B breaks away from his defensive position and attacks player D. A moves into the defensive position of B. Directly after his pass to D, C overlaps D. As soon as he is in line with the player, C plays the ball into his path. Now B follows the ball-carrying player D, and A moves farther sideways and considerably backwards so that he can intervene at any time. The defenders don't participate in the attackers' change of positions, but exclusively hand over one player to the other. The exercise ends as soon as the defenders are outplayed.

Equipment:
One goal

Tips:
- At the start, the striker should only run at a moderate pace towards the defenders in order to give them the greatest chance possible to synchronize their runs.
- The speed should be increased little by little.
- The lateral distance between the players at the start should be approximately 7-12m.
- The players stand opposite each other approximately 15m apart.
- Defender A stands approximately 5m off-center behind player B.
- C overlaps D as soon as the ball leaves his foot.
- Be aware this is a precise and powerful passing play.

Field size:
20 x 20 m

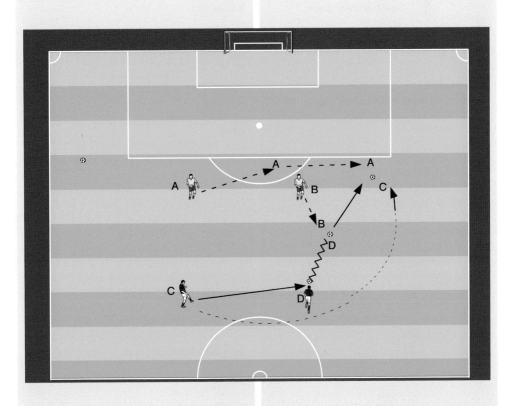

Training Target
- Tactics

Training Emphasis
- Four man backfield

Training Aspects

Skills involved:	Defensive/Offensive play, Speed of movement with ball, Quick anticipation, Outside of the foot, Controlling the ball, One touch passes, Dribbling, Quick decisions, Overlapping, Inside of the foot, Combining technical skill with movement, Body fake, Pushing
Age level:	13-14 years, 15 years to Adult, Under 12, Under 13
Level of play:	Beginner
Type of training:	Group training
Training structure:	Progression, Main point/Emphasis
Purpose:	Defensive behaviors, Attack behaviors, Improve individual qualities
Total number of players:	4 or more players
Participating players:	Whole team
Training location:	Any
Dealing with space:	Half field
Duration:	10-15 min
Physiology:	Soccer-specific endurance, Power & Speed

Organization:
Four players (blue A and B defenders/ red C and D attackers) are positioned on the field according to the diagram. The ball is with player D.

Completing the drill:
The exercise starts with a pass from player C to player D, who immediately starts to dribble forward. Simultaneously, player B breaks away from his defensive position and attacks player D. A moves into the defensive position of B. Directly after his pass to D, C overlaps D. D dribbles diagonally to the left in a central position. B stays with player D. A intersects behind B and orients himself towards player C. As soon as the player is in the penalty area, the drill is over.

Equipment:
One goal.

Tips:
- In contrast to the exercise "2 on 2 – engage with handover" the defenders participate here in the attackers' changing of positions, as this drill takes place in a goal scoring area and "handing over" can lead to a speedrary shooting opportunity for the ball-carrying attacker.
- This exercise is a dry run. No tackling takes place. The primary function of the exercise is the learning of paths in soccer.
- The exercise should be repeatedly trained as many times as possible (to ensure automatic movement sequences).
- Be aware this is a precise and powerful passing play.

- The start signal for the counter reaction is when the passer of the ball moves to pass.
- The lateral distance between the players at the starting position should consist of approximately 7-12m. The pair of players stand opposite each other with a distance of 15m between them.

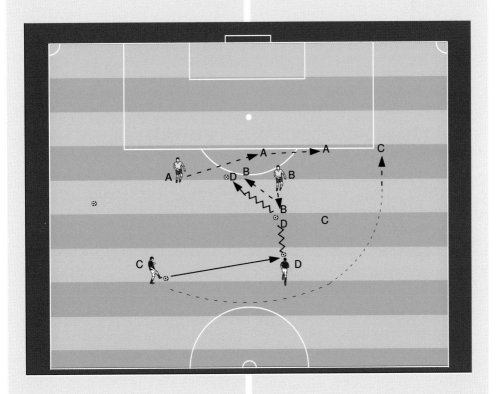

Training Target
- **Tactics**

Training Emphasis
- **Four man backfield**

Training Aspects

Skills involved:	Defensive play
Age level:	13-14 years, 15 years to Adult, Under 12, Under 13
Level of play:	Beginner
Type of training:	Group training
Training structure:	Progression, Main point/Emphasis
Purpose:	Defensive behaviors
Total number of players:	3 players
Participating players:	Whole team
Training location:	Any
Dealing with space:	Half field
Duration:	5 min

Organization:
Three players (blue A, B and C defenders) are positioned on the field according to the diagram.

Completing the drill:
The players line up in the basic formation of a back three (so in a line) in order to get a feel for the distance to one another.

Equipment:
One goal

Tips:
- This exercise is a static dry run and helps in the learning and understanding of the distances between each other.
- The learning of the back three formation is a preparatory exercise for learning player behavior in the back four.
- The distances between players A, B and C amount to 7-12 meters each.

Field size:
30 x 20 m

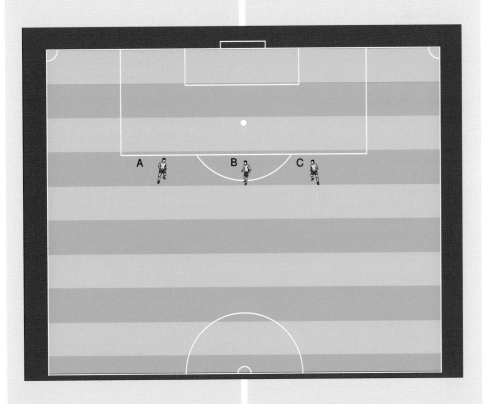

Training Target
- **Tactics**

Training Emphasis
- **Four man backfield**

Training Aspects

Skills involved:	Defensive play, Quick anticipation, Trapping, Inside of the foot passing, Inside of the laces passing, Long passing, Pushing
Age level:	13-14 years, 15 years to Adult, Under 12, Under 13
Level of play:	Beginner
Type of training:	Group training
Training structure:	Progression, Main point/Emphasis
Purpose:	Defensive behaviors
Total number of players:	4 or more players
Participating players:	Whole team
Training location:	Any
Dealing with space:	Half field
Duration:	5-15 min
Physiology:	Soccer-specific endurance

Organization:
The three defenders A, B and C move out of the basic formation of the back three (aligned) into the final position shown in the diagram. The ball is with player D.

Completing the drill:
Player D passes the ball diagonally to the right. The players start from the basic position and move into the final position that is shown in the diagram. This means that player C moves to the ball and stops it, B moves laterally behind C, and A moves laterally behind B. After every passage the players line up anew in the starting position and the procedure starts again.

Tips:
- This exercise is a dry run without tackling. Its primary function is the rehearsing/studying of paths in soccer.
- In the basic formation, the players stand in line. The distance between the players amounts to 7-12m across. If the players play deep, the distance between them in depth is approximately 5 meters, the distance across remains the same.
- Player C runs at the highest speed to the ball. The two defenders constantly uphold the distance.
- The exercise should be trained as many times as possible (to ensure automatic movement sequences).
- The signal for the initiation of the paths is the keeper of the ball moving to pass.

Field size:
50 x 40 m

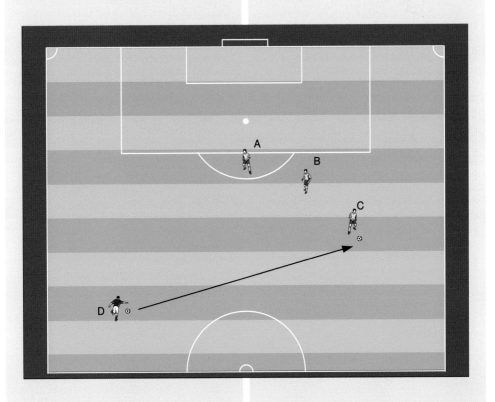

Training Target
- **Tactics**

Training Emphasis
- **Four man backfield**

Training Aspects

Skills involved:	Defensive play, Quick anticipation, Trapping, Quick decisions, Inside of the laces passing, Long passing, Pushing
Age level:	13-14 years, 15 years to Adult, Under 12, Under 13
Level of play:	Beginner
Type of training:	Group training
Training structure:	Progression, Main point/Emphasis
Purpose:	Defensive behaviors
Total number of players:	4 or more players
Participating players:	Whole team
Training location:	Any
Dealing with space:	Half field
Duration:	10-15 min
Physiology:	Soccer-specific endurance

Organization:
The three defenders A, B and C move out of the basic formation of the back three (aligned) into the final position shown in the diagram. The ball is with player D.

Completing the drill:
Player D passes the ball diagonally to the left. The players start from the basic position and move into the final position that is shown in the diagram. This means that player A moves to the ball and stops it, B moves laterally behind A, and C moves laterally behind B. After ever passage the players line up anew in the starting position and the procedure starts again.

Tips:
- This exercise is a dry run without tackling. Its primary function is the rehearsing/studying of paths in soccer.
- In the basic formation the players stand in line. The distance between the players amounts to 7-12m across. When the players play deep, the distance in depth is approximately 5 meters, the distance across remains the same.
- Player A runs at the highest speed to the ball. The two defenders constantly uphold the distance.
- The exercise should be trained as many times as possible (to ensure automatic movement sequences).
- The signal for the initiation of the play is the keeper of the ball moving to pass.

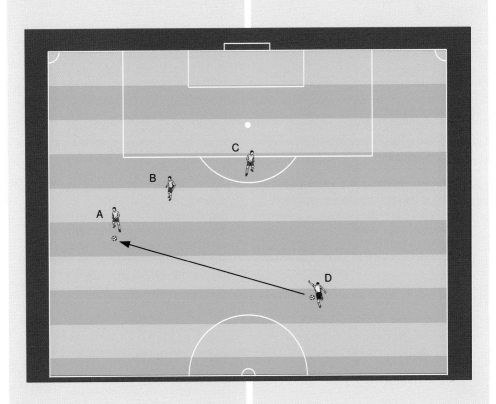

Training Target
- Tactics

Training Emphasis
- Four man backfield

Training Aspects

Skills involved:	Defensive play, Quick anticipation, Trapping, Quick decisions, Short passing, Pushing
Age level:	13-14 years, 15 years to Adult, Under 12, Under 13
Level of play:	Beginner
Type of training:	Group training
Training structure:	Progression
Purpose:	Defensive behaviors
Total number of players:	4 or more players
Participating players:	Whole team
Training location:	Any
Dealing with space:	Half field
Duration:	5-15 min
Physiology:	Soccer-specific endurance

Organization:
The three blue defenders A, B and C move out of the basic back three formation (aligned) into the final position (triangular formation) shown in the diagram. The ball is with player D.

Completing the drill:
Player D passes the ball in the center to player B. The central defender B then moves out towards the ball. At the same time, players A and C engage and safeguard player B. When the final position has been reached and the distances are correct, the players go back into the basic position and the procedure starts anew.

Tips:
- This exercise is a dry run without tackling. Its primary function is the rehearsing/studying of paths in soccer.
- In the basic formation, the players stand in line. The distance between the players amounts to 7-12m across. If the central defender advances and the two wingbacks play deep, the distances in depth between the central defender and wingbacks will be approximately 8-10 meters. The distance between the two wingbacks comes to approximately 7 meters.
- Central defender B runs at the highest speed to the ball and attempts to get to it at the earliest possible moment.
- The signal for the initiation of running the paths is the keeper of the ball moving to pass.

Field size:
50 x 40 m

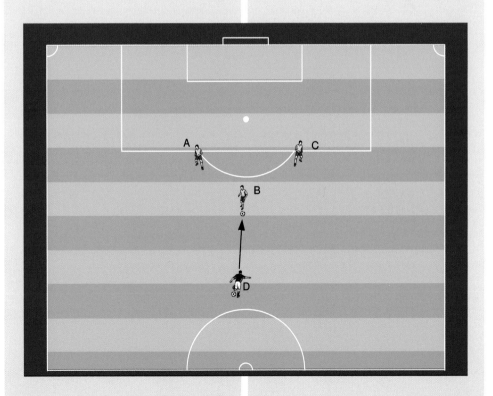

Organization:

The players are positioned in a basic 4-4-2 formation (aligned) in accordance with the diagram. Doing this can cause some players to have multiple duties. Every player, or position, is assigned a letter.

Completing the drill:

The players line up in the basic back four formation (i.e. in lines) in order to get a feel for the distances between each other.

Tips:

- This exercise is a static dry run and serves to teach and aid in understanding the distances to be kept from one another.
- The learning of the back four system is a basic requirement for learning the different paths in the back four and therefore represents the basis for all other 4-4-2 exercises.

- The distances between each player across amounts to 7-12 meters, and approximately 10-12 meters in depth.

The basic formation corresponds to the 4-4-2 defensive formation practiced in the basic zone defense. At the same time it means that when an opposition player enters a defending player's zone he is to be taken and that in this zone there should be no "handing over" of players. If an opposition player comes into a goal-scoring area, the players are marked man-to-man, as when "handing over" players short spaces of time can emerge where the opponent is not being marked.
It is left up to the coach himself whether he switches to man-to-man marking instead of zone defense in dead ball situations. Both options have their advantages and disadvantages.

Basic formation:
GK = Goalkeeper
A = Left back
B = Left central defender
C = Right central defender
D = Right back

E = Left midfielder
F = Left halfback midfielder
G = Right halfback midfielder
H = Right midfielder
I = Left striker
J = Right striker

Training Target
- Tactics

Training Emphasis
- Four man backfield

Training Aspects

Skills involved:	Defensive play
Age level:	13 - 14 years, 15 years to Adult, Under 12, Under 13
Level of play:	Beginner
Type of training:	Group training
Training structure:	Progression, Main point/Emphasis
Purpose:	Defensive behaviors
Total number of players:	4 or more players
Participating players:	Whole team
Training location:	Any
Dealing with space:	Half field
Duration:	5 min
Physiology:	Soccer-specific endurance

Organization:
Four players (blue A, B, C and D defenders) are positioned on the playing field according to the diagram

Completing the drill:
The players position themselves in the basic back four formation. The distances between the players A, B, C and D amount to between 7-12 meters each.

Field size:
40 x 30 m

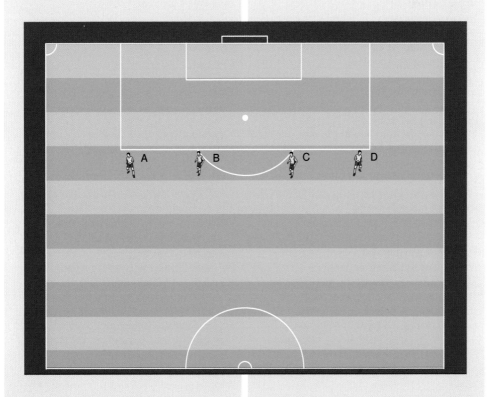

Training Target
- Tactics

Training Emphasis
- Four man backfield

Training Aspects

Skills involved:	Defensive play, Quick anticipation, Trapping, Quick decisions, Inside of the foot passing, Long passing, Pushing
Age level:	13-14 years, 15 years to Adult, Under 12, Under 13
Level of play:	Beginner
Type of training:	Group training
Training structure:	Warm-up, Progression, Main point/Emphasis
Purpose:	Defensive behaviors
Total number of players:	5 players
Participating players:	Whole team
Training location:	Any
Dealing with space:	Half field
Duration:	5-15 min
Physiology:	Soccer-specific endurance

Organization:
The four defenders A, B, C and D move out of the basic back four formation (aligned) into the position shown in the diagram, which resembles a crescent. Player E has the ball. Positions can be multi-occupied without problems.

Completing the drill:
Player E passes the ball right in the direction of the left back/direction of the touchline. At the moment the player moves to strike the ball, the left back D runs forward in the direction of the ball and stops it. At the same time, the other defenders move as follows: Player C marches out forward and safeguards D; Player B moves parallel to the edge of the penalty box to the left until he's approximately even with the first post while player A moves until he's even with the second post, and approximately even with player B or 1 to 2 meters in front. When the players have taken up their final positions and the distances between them is correct,

the players go back to their starting positions and the exercise starts anew.

Equipment:
One goal

Tips:
- This exercise is a dry run. No tackling takes place. Its main function is the learning of paths in soccer.
- The exercise should be trained as many times as possible to ensure automatic movement sequences.
- The lateral distance between the players is 7-12 meters.
- The distances in depth in the final position between D, C and B is approximately 8-10 meters each.
- The final position is crescent-shaped.
- The signal for initiating the paths is the keeper of the ball moving to strike the ball.
- The wingback D runs at the highest speed to the ball and attempts to reach it at the earliest possible moment.

Field size:
Half a playing field

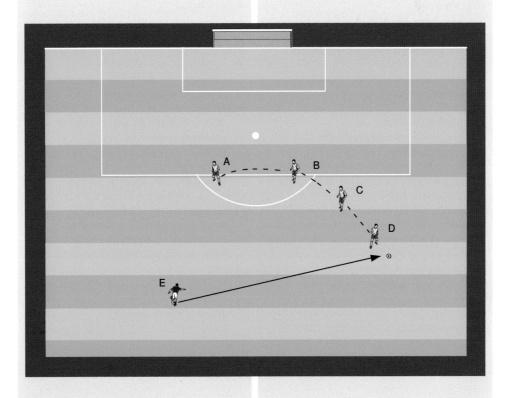

Training Target
- **Tactics**

Training Emphasis
- **Four man backfield**

Training Aspects

Skills involved:	Defensive play, Quick anticipation, Trapping, Quick decisions, Inside of the laces passing, Long passing, Pushing
Age level:	13-14 years, 15 years to Adult, Under 12, Under 13
Level of play:	Beginner
Type of training:	Group training
Training structure:	Progression, Main point/Emphasis
Purpose:	Defensive behaviors
Total number of players:	5 players
Participating players:	Whole team
Training location:	Any
Dealing with space:	Half field
Duration:	5-15 min
Physiology:	Soccer-specific endurance

Organization:
The four defenders A, B, C and D move out of the basic back four formation (aligned) into the position shown in the diagram, which resembles a crescent. Player E has the ball. Positions can be multi-occupied without problems.

Completing the drill:
Player E passes the ball left in the direction of the right back/direction of the touchline. At the moment the player moves to strike the ball, the right back A runs forward in the direction of the ball and stops it. At the same time, the other defenders move as follows: Player B marches out forward and safeguards A; Player C moves parallel to the edge of the penalty box to the left, until he's approximately even with the first post while player D moves until he's even with the second post, approximately even with player C or 1 to 2 meters in front. When the players have taken up their final positions and the distances between them is correct, the players go back to their starting positions and the exercise starts anew.

Equipment:
One goal.

Tips:
- This exercise is a dry run. No tackling takes place. Its main function is the learning of paths in soccer.
- The exercise should be trained as many times as possible to ensure automatic movement sequences.
- The lateral distance between the players is 7-12 meters.
- The distances in depth in the final position between A, B and C is approximately 8-10 meters each.
- The final position is crescent-shaped.
- The signal for initiating the paths is the keeper of the ball moving to strike the ball.
- The wingback D runs at the highest speed to the ball and attempts to reach it at the earliest possible moment.

Field size:
50 x 40 m

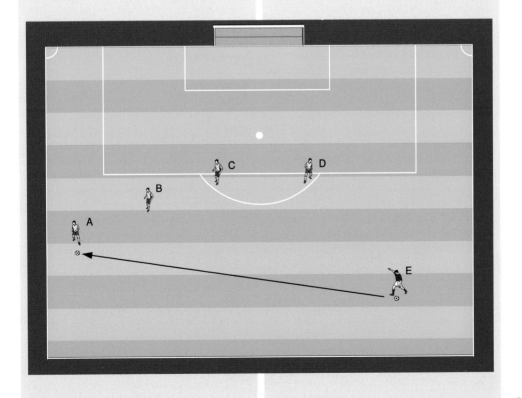

Training Target
- Tactics

Training Emphasis
- Four man backfield

Training Aspects

Skills involved:	Defensive play, Quick anticipation, Trapping, Quick decisions, Inside of the laces passing, Long passing, Pushing
Age level:	13-14 years, 15 years to Adult, Under 12, Under 13
Level of play:	Beginner
Type of training:	Group training
Training structure:	Progression, Main point/Emphasis
Purpose:	Defensive behaviors
Total number of players:	8 or more players
Participating players:	Whole team
Training location:	Any
Dealing with space:	Half field
Duration:	5-15 min
Physiology:	Soccer-specific endurance
Goal keeping:	1 goalie

Organization:
The four defenders A, B, C and D move out of the basic back four formation (aligned) into the final position shown in the diagram, which resembles a crescent. The two red attackers G and H act as strikers, E and F as wide midfielders. Player E has the ball.

Completing the drill:
The ball is passed by player E to the left attacking side to player F. Defender A, who is responsible for this zone, advances out of the basic formation and attacks F. As the strikers are standing in this situation near the central defenders in a potential goal-scoring area and there is a threat of a direct cross from F, the central defenders assign themselves the strikers and simply retreat somewhat into a deep position. Player D moves in line with the second post, approximately even with player C. Player F is now working the ball and attempts to put a direct cross into the penalty area. The two strikers attempt to score a goal and player E

runs diagonally into the penalty area, where he is assisted by D, and also attempts to salvage the ball.

Equipment:
One goal

Tips:
- The defensive line stands about 22-23 meters in front of the goal in the basic formation and the lateral distance between the defenders is about 7-12 meters.
- The signal for initiating the paths is the keeper of the ball moving to strike the ball.
- Defender A runs at the highest speed to player F and attempts to challenge him at the earliest possible moment. At the same time, the defensive players drop 5-6 meters deeper.
- The diagonal cross from E should be played to the inner post, allowing the ball

to have high speed and a straight line to the goal.

- E sprints diagonally in the direction of the penalty area after his pass.
- The strikers can cross over.

Field size:
Half a playing field

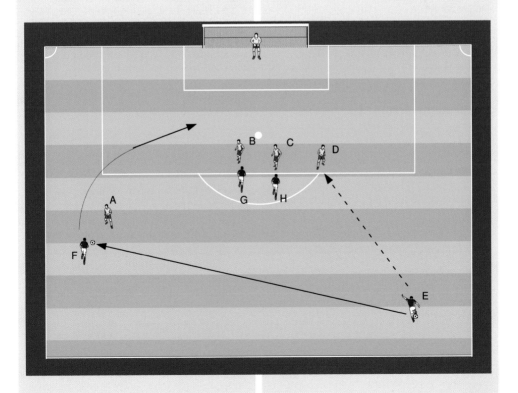

Training Target
- **Tactics**

Training Emphasis
- **Four man backfield**

Training Aspects

Skills involved:	Defensive play, Quick anticipation, Trapping, Quick decisions, Inside of the laces passing, Long passing, Pushing
Age level:	13-14 years, 15 years to Adult, Under 12, Under 13
Level of play:	Beginner
Type of training:	Group training
Training structure:	Progression, Main point/Emphasis
Purpose:	Defensive behaviors
Total number of players:	9 players
Participating players:	Whole team
Training location:	Any
Dealing with space:	Half field
Duration:	5-15 min
Physiology:	Soccer-specific endurance

Organization:
The four players blue A, B, C, D, along with X defenders/red E, F, G and H attackers move out of the basic formation on the playing field into the final position shown in the diagram. Player E has the ball.

Completing the drill:
Behaving and moving with ball-orientated zone defense.

Variants:
Two strikers stand close to the central defenders in the potential goal-scoring area.

Alternative formation, or alternative paths/sliding scale of the back four (engaging, shifting) happens when the ball is played from the opponent player E to the left side of attack in the area/zone to player F while the two strikers are standing in the middle near the goal.

Player D moves up to the second post, approximately even with player C. Player C assigns himself the opposing striker H and player B assigns himself the striker G. A attacks F, who has he ball.

Equipment:
One goal.

Tips:
This setup applies when the outer left midfielder has enough time to move up and isn't bound to another opponent.

Field size:
Half a playing field

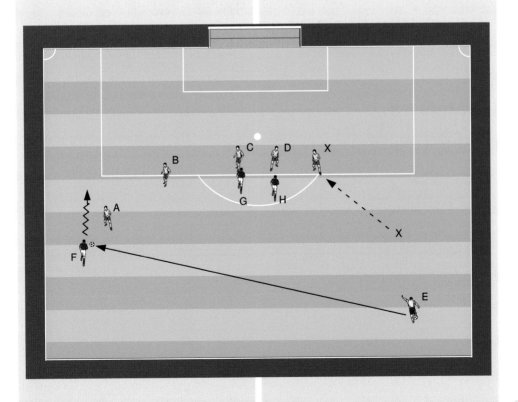

Training Target
- Tactics

Training Emphasis
- Four man backfield

Training Aspects

Skills involved:	Defensive play, Quick anticipation, Trapping, Quick decisions, Inside of the laces passing, Short passing, Pushing
Age level:	13-14 years, 15 years to Adult, Under 12, Under 13
Level of play:	Beginner
Type of training:	Group training
Training structure:	Progression, Main point/Emphasis
Purpose:	Defensive behaviors
Total number of players:	5 players
Participating players:	Whole team
Training location:	Any
Dealing with space:	Half field
Duration:	5-15 min
Physiology:	Soccer-specific endurance

Organization:
The four blue defenders A, B, C and D position themselves in the back four basic formation (aligned). Player E has the ball. The positions can be multi-occupied without any problems.

Completing the drill:
Player E starts to dribble in the direction of the left side central defender C. C moves out of the linear formation and attacks E. At the same time, D and B move sideways to safeguard player C. Player A moves sideways to the left until he's in line with the front post. If player C apprehends player E and the distances between the players are correct, the players go back to their starting positions and the exercise starts anew.

Equipment:
One goal.

Tips:
- This exercise is a dry run. There is no tackling. Its primary function is the learning of paths in soccer.
- The exercise should be trained as many times as possible to ensure automatic movement sequences.
- The lateral distance between the players is approximately 7-12 meters.
- The distance in depth in the final position (from C to A, B and D) is approximately 8-10 meters.
- The movement of the right side central defender B and the left back D behind player C leads to the formation of a defensive triangle.
- The signal for initiating the play is the keeper of the ball moving to strike the ball.

Field size:
Half a playing field

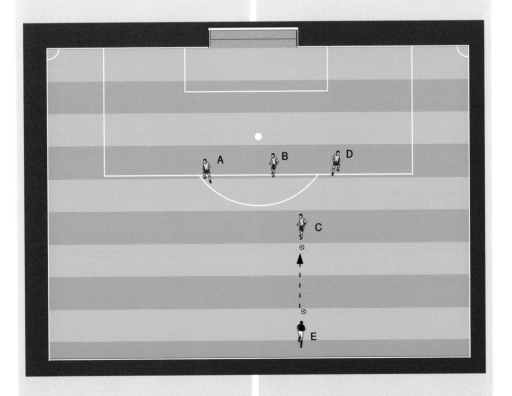

Training Target
- Tactics

Training Emphasis
- Four man backfield

Training Aspects

Skills involved:	Defensive play, Quick anticipation, Trapping, Quick decisions, Inside of the foot passing, Short passing, Pushing
Age level:	13-14 years, 15 years to Adult, Under 12, Under 13
Level of play:	Beginner
Type of training:	Group training
Training structure:	Progression, Main point/Emphasis
Purpose:	Defensive behaviors
Total number of players:	5 players
Participating players:	Whole team
Training location:	Any
Dealing with space:	Half field
Duration:	5-15 min
Physiology:	Soccer-specific endurance

Organization:
The four blue defenders A, B, C and D position themselves in the back four basic formation (aligned). Player E has the ball. The positions can be multi-occupied without any problems.

Completing the drill:
Player E starts to dribble in the direction of the right side central defender B. B moves out of the linear formation and attacks E. At the same time, C and A move sideways to safeguard B. D moves sideways to the left until he's in line with the first post. If player B apprehends player E and the distances between the players are correct, the players go back to their starting positions and the exercise starts anew.

Equipment:
One goal.

Tips:
- This exercise is a dry run. There is no tackling. Its primary function is the learning of paths in soccer.
- The exercise should be trained as many times as possible to ensure automatic movement sequences.
- The lateral distance between the players is approximately 7-12 meters.
- The distance in depth in the final position (from C to A, B and D) is approximately 8-10 meters.
- The movement of the right side central defender B and the left back D behind player C leads to the formation of a defensive triangle.
- The signal for initiating the play is the keeper of the ball moving to strike the ball.

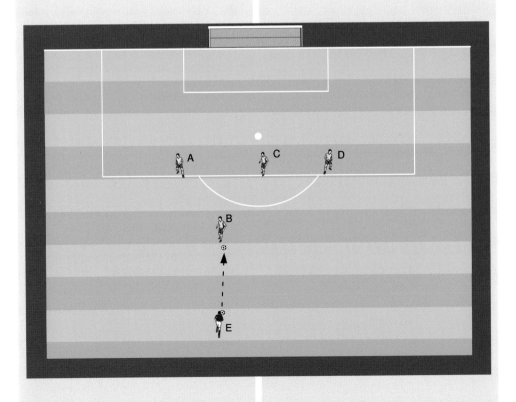

Training Target
- **Tactics**

Training Emphasis
- **Four man backfield**

Training Aspects

Skills involved:	Quick anticipation, Trapping, Quick decisions, Inside of the foot passing, Inside of the laces passing, Long passing, Pushing
Age level:	13-14 years, 15 years to Adult, Under 12, Under 13
Level of play:	Beginner
Type of training:	Group training
Training structure:	Progression, Main point/Emphasis
Purpose:	Defensive behaviors
Total number of players:	5 players
Participating players:	Whole team
Training location:	Any
Dealing with space:	Half field
Duration:	5-15 min
Physiology:	Soccer-specific endurance

Organization:
The four defenders A, B, C and D position themselves in the back four basic formation (aligned). Player E has the ball.

Completing the drill:
Player E plays a deep pass from the left-hand side of attack through the gap between the right back A and the right side central defender B. Now the closest placed central defender C must run for the ball. When C has the ball under control, he goes back to his position and the exercise starts anew.

Equipment:
One goal.

Tips:
- This exercise is a dry run. There is no tackling. Its primary function is the learning of paths in soccer.
- The exercise should be trained as many times as possible to ensure automatic movement sequences.
- The focus lies solely on the path of the left side central defender. He should be aware that in a similar situation during a game he must run this path without much time to react, as players A and B can only react after some delay (as they still must turn around).
- In the basic formation, the lateral distance between the players is 7-12 meters.
- C starts as soon as the ball is played from E and it is likely that it will go through the gap between the players.

Field size:
Half a playing field

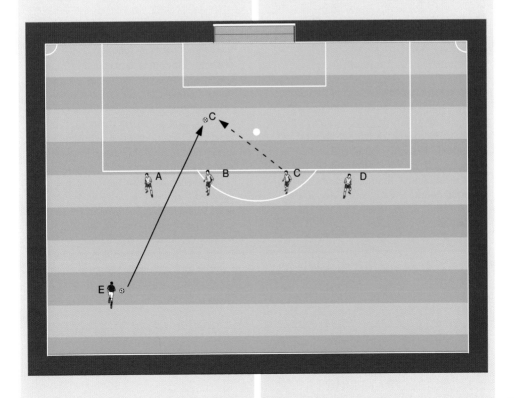

Training Target
- Tactics

Training Emphasis
- Four man backfield

Training Aspects

Skills involved:	Defensive play, Quick anticipation, Trapping, Quick decisions, Inside of the foot passing, Inside of the laces passing, Long passing, Pushing
Age level:	13-14 years, 15 years to Adult, Under 12, Under 13
Level of play:	Beginner
Type of training:	Group training
Training structure:	Progression, Main point/Emphasis
Purpose:	Defensive behaviors
Total number of players:	5 players
Participating players:	Whole team
Training location:	Any
Dealing with space:	Free space
Duration:	10-15 min
Physiology:	Soccer-specific endurance

Organization:
The four defenders A, B, C and D position themselves in the back four basic formation (aligned). Player E has the ball.

Completing the drill:
Player E plays a deep pass from the right-hand side of attack through the gap between the left back D and the left side central defender C. Now the closest placed central defender B must run for the ball. When B has the ball under control, he goes back to his position and the exercise starts anew.

Equipment:
One goal.

Tips:
- This exercise is a dry run. There is no tackling. Its primary function is the learning of paths in soccer.
- The exercise should be trained as many times as possible to ensure automatic movement sequences.
- The focus lies solely on the path of the right side central defender. He should be aware that in a similar situation during a game he must run this path without much time to react, as the players C and D can only react after some delay (as they still must turn around).
- In the basic formation, the lateral distance between the players is 7-12 meters.
- B starts as soon as the ball is played from E and it is likely that it will go through the gap between the players.

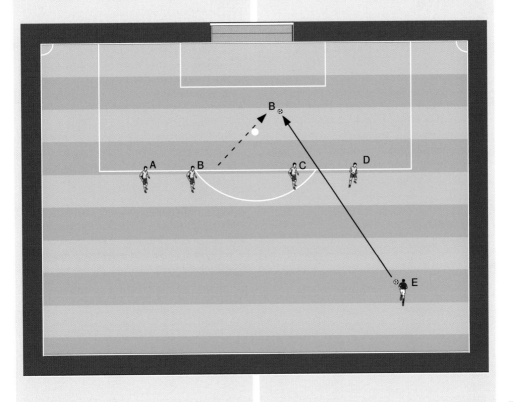

Training Target
- **Tactics**

Training Emphasis
- **Four man backfield**

Training Aspects

Skills involved:	Defensive play, Quick anticipation, Trapping, Quick decisions, Inside of the laces passing, Long passing, Pushing
Age level:	13-14 years, 15 years to Adult, Under 12, Under 13
Level of play:	Beginner
Type of training:	Group training
Training structure:	Progression, Main point/Emphasis
Purpose:	Defensive behaviors
Total number of players:	5 players
Participating players:	Whole team
Training location:	Any
Dealing with space:	Half field
Duration:	5-15 min
Physiology:	Soccer-specific endurance

Organization:
The four defenders A, B, C and D position themselves in the back four basic formation (aligned). Player E has the ball.

Completing the drill:
Player E plays a deep diagonal pass from the right-hand side of attack through the gap between the right and left side central defenders B and C. Now the closest placed to the ball wingback A must run for the ball. When A has the ball under control, he goes back to his position and the exercise starts anew.

Equipment:
One goal.

Tips:
- This exercise is a dry run. There is no tackling. Its primary function is the learning of paths in soccer.
- The exercise should be trained as many times as possible to ensure automatic movement sequences.
- The focus lies solely on the path of the right back. He should be aware that in a similar situation during a game he must run this path without much time to react, as the players B and C can only react after some delay (as they still must turn around).
- In the basic formation, the lateral distance between the players is 7-12 meters.
- A starts as soon as the ball is played from E and it is likely that it will go through the gap between the players.

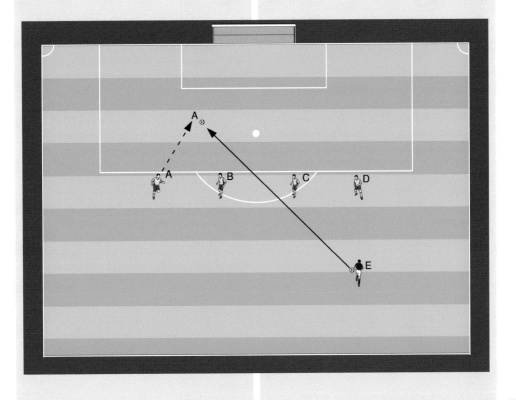

Training Target
- **Tactics**

Training Emphasis
- **Four man backfield**

Training Aspects

Skills involved:	Defensive play, Quick anticipation, Trapping, Quick decisions, Inside of the laces passing, Long passing
Age level:	13-14 years, 15 years to Adult, Under 12, Under 13
Level of play:	Beginner
Type of training:	Group training
Training structure:	Progression, Main point/Emphasis
Purpose:	Defensive behaviors
Total number of players:	5 players
Participating players:	Whole team
Training location:	Any
Dealing with space:	Half field
Duration:	5-15 min
Physiology:	Soccer-specific endurance

Organization:
The four defenders A, B, C and D position themselves in the back four basic formation (aligned). Player E has the ball.

Completing the drill:
Player E plays a deep diagonal pass from the right-hand side of attack through the gap between the right and left side central defenders B and C. Now the player closest the ball, left back D, must run for the ball. When D has the ball under control, he goes back to his position and the exercise starts anew.

Equipment:
One goal.

Tips:
- This exercise is a dry run. There is no tackling. Its primary function is the learning of paths in soccer.
- The exercise should be trained as many times as possible to ensure automatic movement sequences.
- The focus lies solely on the path of the left back. He should be aware that in a similar situation during a game he must run this path without much time to react, as the players B and C can only react after some delay (as they still must turn around).
- In the basic formation, the lateral distance between the players is 7-12 meters.
- D starts as soon as the ball is played from E and it is likely that it will go through the gap between the players.

Field size:
Half a playing field

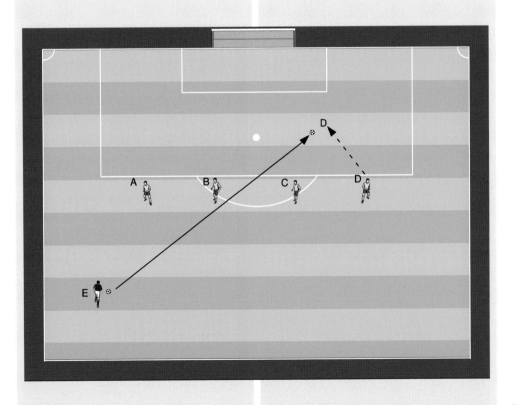

Training Target
- Tactics

Training Emphasis
- Four man backfield

Training Aspects

Training structure:	Main point/Emphasis
Duration:	1-10 min

Organization:
Using cones on the touchline, the "stand deep/drop pressing zone" is marked from the edge of the penalty box up to the semi-circle on the halfway line.

Completing the drill:
The pressing zone shown here, in comparison to the defensive, midfield and attacking pressing zones, is the most defensive of the four pressing zones. In this zone, as the name has already revealed, the players stand, or indeed play, deepest. All outfield players in the 4-4-2 formation find themselves in this zone during the defensive pressing play. The task of every single player in this zone is to defend the area allocated to him according to his position. He will attack the opponent in his zone by going to him, and if the opponent leaves the zone, the defender automatically drops back into the deep lying start position.

Exception:
The opponent runs into a potential goal scoring area. In this situation he must continue to attack with the purpose of preventing his opponent from shooting on goal.

Field size:
Whole playing field

Cone distance:
The complete width of the field.

Length:
30-35 m

Training Target
- **Tactics**

Training Emphasis
- **Four man backfield**

Training Aspects

	Main point/Emphasis
Training structure:	
Duration:	1-10 min

Organization:
Using cones on the touchline, the defensive pressing zone is marked from the edge of the penalty box up to the halfway line.

Completing the drill:
The pressing zone shown here, in comparison to the midfield and attacking pressing zones, is one of the most defensive of the four pressing zones. In this one, as the name has already revealed, a defensive pressing game is played. All outfield players in the 4-4-2 formation find themselves in this zone during the defensive pressing play. The task of every single player in this zone is to defend the area allocated to him according to his position.

Field size:
Whole playing field

Cone distance:
The complete width of the field

Length:
30-35 m

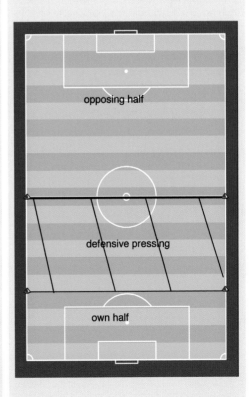

Training Target
- **Tactics**

Training Emphasis
- **Four man backfield**

Training Aspects

Training structure:	Main point/Emphasis
Duration:	1-10 min

Organization:
Using cones placed on the touchline, the midfield pressing zone is marked. The zone covers the area 1-2 meters behind the center circle of the team's own half to 1-2 meters in front of the center circle in the opponent's half.

Completing the drill:
The pressing zone here, in comparison to the defensive and attacking pressing zones, represents the central pressing zone. In this zone, as the name suggests, a midfield pressing game is played. All outfield players in the 4-4-2 formation find themselves in this zone during the midfield pressing play. The task of every single player in this zone is to defend the area allocated to him according to his position.

Field size:
Whole playing field

Cone distance:
The complete width of the field

Length:
30-35 m

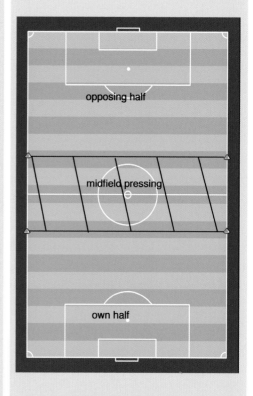

Training Target
- **Tactics**

Training Emphasis
- **Four man backfield**

Training Aspects

Training structure:	**Main point/Emphasis**
Duration:	**1-10 min**

Organization:
Using cones placed on the touchline, the attacking pressing zone is marked. The zone covers the area from the halfway line up to 5 meters in front of the semicircle of the opponent's penalty area.

Completing the drill:
The pressing zone here, in comparison to the defensive and midfield pressing zones, is the most offensive pressing zone. In this zone, as the name suggests, an attacking pressing game (also called fore checking) is played. All outfield players in the 4-4-2 formation find themselves in this zone during the attacking pressing play. The task of every single player in this zone is to occupy the area allocated to him according to his position, in order to seize possession of the ball as a result of the team's clever shifting and movement to the ball.

Field size:
Whole playing field

Cone distance:
The complete width of the field

Length:
30-35 m

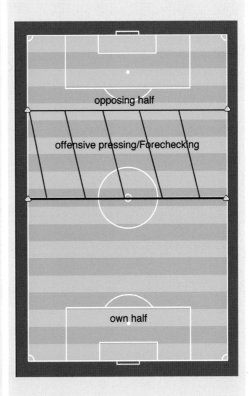

Training Target
- **Tactics**

Training Emphasis
- **Four man backfield**

Training Aspects

Training structure:	Progression, Main point/Emphasis
Duration:	1-10 min

Organization:
10 players and 1 goalkeeper are positioned on the playing field as shown in the diagram. A letter is assigned to each player (or position). The positions can be multi-occupied without any problems.

Field size:
Whole playing field

Completing the drill:
The players are positioned in a 4-4-2 formation and subdivided into pairs. The distance across is between 7-12 meters (e.g., between B and C) and between 10-15 meters in depth (e.g., between B and F). The players who are outlined in a rectangle form a pair and are responsible for safeguarding each other in the game.

Tips:
This exercise represents a purely static dry run. The players should get a feel on the field for their respective positions to one another. The players should get an explanation from the coach (on a tactic board at best) before the training session about the importance of the formation and their respective positions and should be prepared for what will be expected from them on the training field. This verbal theoretical introduction is then followed by the execution on the field, which aids in the visualization and execution of the verbal explanations.

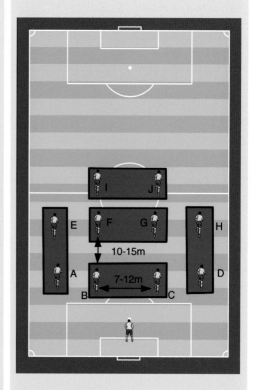

Training Target
- **Tactics**

Training Emphasis
- **Four man backfield**

Training Aspects

Training structure:	Progression, Main point/Emphasis
Duration:	1-10 min

Organization:
The player is in his position on the field (1).

Field size:
Whole playing field

Completing the drill:
In this exercise, the paths of the right side outer midfielder, or the right wing, when the opposition has possession, and when he himself has possession, are presented. Depending on the position of the ball when the opposition has possession, the path of the player runs in a diagonal line from his original position (1) via position 2 into an indented defensive position (3). The opposite running direction 3—›1 corresponds to the path when switching from the opposition having possession to his own team coming into possession of the ball.

Tips:
- This exercise is a dry run. There is no tackling. Its main function is the learning of paths in soccer.
- The drill should be trained as many times as possible to ensure automatic movement sequences.
- The focus lies solely on the right midfielder's path. He should be aware that in a similar situation during a game he must run this path without much time to react.
- The individual positions (1-3) can also be marked out with cones. In this situation, the player run into the individual positions according to the shouts or balls played by the coach/teammates.
- The paths should always be run at a high speed.

Training Target
- **Tactics**

Training Emphasis
- **Four man backfield**

Training Aspects

Training structure:	Progression, Main point/Emphasis
Duration:	1-10 min

Organization:
The team is positioned on the field in a defensive basic formation of the 4-4-2 in the defensive pressing zone. The team positions itself into the final positions shown in the picture. The ball serves as the point of orientation for the players. The positions can be multi-occupied without any problems.

Completing the drill:
The aim is to illustrate that the whole team moves solely in an area of 30-35 meters across and deep when the opponent has possession of the ball. Therefore room for the opponent is made tight and the opposing team can be aggressively put under pressure. With this form of shifting and moving up, triangles are always formed (as shown in the picture). Through the formation of triangles, a mutual safeguarding and restriction of space emerge. As a result, the opponent finds it difficult to force through a pass or dribble. In the depicted example, the ball is located in a central position in front of the right halfback midfielder G. The two other players near the ball, midfielders F and H, move behind G (shadow covering) and the striker J blocks the path of the player with the ball. The other players shift likewise in the direction of the ball.

Tips:
- This exercise is a dry run. There is no tackling. Its main function is the learning of paths used in soccer and the formation of triangles.
- The drill should be trained as many times as possible to ensure automatic movement sequences.
- The focus lies solely on the paths of the players and the collective, on each other coordinated exercise. The players should

be aware that in a similar situation during a game they must run these learned paths without much time to think.
- In the basic formation, the lateral distances between the players are 7-12 meters.
- The offset in depth inside the triangles is 8-10 meters.
- The players must continually communicate and amend the play where applicable.

Field size:
Whole playing field

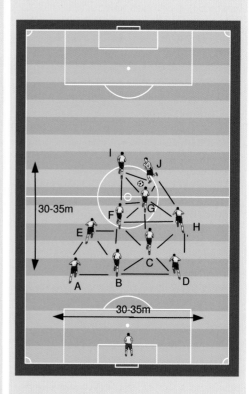

Training Target
- **Tactics**

Training Emphasis
- **Four man backfield**

Training Aspects

Training structure:	Progression, Main point/Emphasis
Duration:	1-10 min

Organization:
The three yellow defenders position themselves in a back three formation (aligned). The blue attacker D (who has the ball) stands facing to the defenders, and directly opposite central defender B. From this position the players then move into the final position shown in the diagram.

Completing the drill:
Player D dribbles out of his starting position in the direction of player B. Player B breaks out from the linear grouping and attacks D. Players A and C are positioned behind B in a triangular formation. The resulting space behind B is called the "shadow cover," as this area is covered for a pass from player D. If player B has arrived even with the ball and the paths and the distances between the players are correct, the players go back to their starting positions and the drill starts anew.

Tips:
- This exercise is a dry run. There is no tackling. Its main function is the learning of paths in soccer.
- The drill should be trained as many times as possible to ensure automatic movement sequences.
- The focus lies solely on the paths of the back three. The players should be aware that in a similar situation during a game they must move into a triangular formation without much time to think.
- The distances between the individual players can vary, depending on speed, change in the game situation, etc., and are normally wide as well as deep in each case 7 to at the most 15 meters from player to player.

- B starts as soon as D starts a dribble. At the same time the two wingbacks move into position.
- The nearer B runs to D, the bigger the shadow cover becomes. This optimizes the prevention of passes behind the defenders, but at the same time enables the attacker to dribble against B, as behind B he would find more time for a follow-up action (e.g., shot on goal) as a result of the larger distance away from the other two defenders

Field size:
20 x 20 m

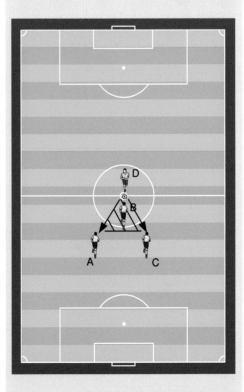

Training Target
- **Tactics**

Training Emphasis
- **Four man backfield**

Training Aspects

Training structure:	Progression, Main point/Emphasis
Duration:	1-10 min

Organization:
The team is positioned on the playing field in the defensive basic 4-4-2 formation in the defensive pressing zone. A player (or the coach) runs with the ball near the right-hand touchline towards the striker. The team shifts to the final position as shown in the picture. The positions can be multi-occupied without problems.

Completing the drill:
The blue player (coach), dribbles with the ball in a central position towards the team. The closest player to the ball (striker I) runs head-on and attacks him. The other players move up as shown, constrict the space and mutually cover for each other.

Tips:
- The players located in a straight extension to the ball in the 4-4-2 formation (I, F, B) leave their linear formation most distinctly forward in comparison to the other players. This ensures that triangular coverage is formed and the direct path to goal is blocked at an early stage (shadow coverage). For better clarification, it may help to compare the ball to a magnet. The players who are positioned in front of the magnet are more strongly "attracted" to it than the others.
- This exercise is a dry run. There is no tackling. Its main function is the learning of paths in soccer.
- The drill should be trained as many times as possible to ensure automatic movement sequences.
- The focus lies solely on the paths of the team using the example of an attacking right side central defender's. The players should be aware that in a similar situation during a game they must be able to implement these paths without much time to react.
- The distance between each player varies depending on the speed of the play, changes in ball possession, etc. Players are usually 7 to 15 meters across and deep from each other.
- The distance in depth inside the triangles is 8-10 meters and 7-12 meters in width between the two players at the back.
- The team acts on a field with dimensions of 30-35 x 30-35 meters.
- In order to be able to exercise neat and effective pressing, strong communication between the players and scrupulous corrections from the coach are needed.

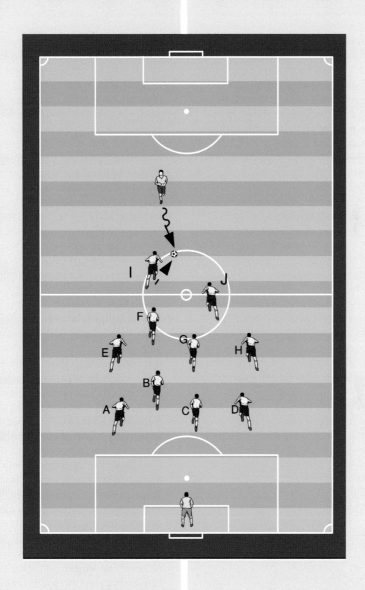

Training Target
- Tactics

Training Emphasis
- Four man backfield

Training Aspects

Training structure:	Progression, Main point/Emphasis
Duration:	1-10 min

Organization:
The team is positioned on the playing field in the defensive basic 4-4-2 formation in the defensive pressing zone. A player (or the coach) runs with the ball near the right-hand touchline towards the striker. The team shifts to the final position as shown in the picture. The positions can be multi-occupied without problems.

Completing the drill:
In contrast to a central attacking player, the player coming down the flanks is run to by the striker closest to the ball (I), who consequently pushes the path into the middle. The second striker (J) can offensively press the ball-carrying player, i.e., block the path to the opposition goalkeeper/defenders, or safeguard the path to pass/run into their own half. The outer left midfielder blocks the way down the sideline and prevents deep forward passes or runs. He double covers the ball-carrying player together with striker I. The defensive and midfield lines shift likewise as shown in the diagram towards the ball (in each case a crescent-shaped alignment of the two rows). If the final position has been achieved and the paths and distances are correct, the players go back to their starting positions and the drill starts anew.

Tips:
- The players located in a straight extension to the ball in the 4-4-2 formation (E and A) leave their linear formation most distinctly forward in comparison to the other players. This ensures that triangular coverage is formed and the direct path to goal is blocked at an early stage (shadow coverage). For better clarification, it may help to compare the ball to a magnet. The players who are positioned in front of the magnet are more strongly "attracted" to it than the others.
- This exercise is a dry run. There is no tackling. Its main function is the learning of paths in soccer.
- The drill should be trained as many times as possible to ensure automatic movement sequences.
- The focus lies solely on the paths of the team. For example, when the play will be different if the attacking right back's path is followed. The players should be aware that in a similar situation during a game they must be able to implement these paths without much time to react.
- The distance between each player varies depending on the speed of the play, changes in ball possession, etc. Players are usually 7 to 15 meters across and deep from each other.
- The distance in depth inside the triangles is 8-10 meters and 7-12 meters in width between the two players at the back.
- The team acts on a field that is 30-35 x 30-35 meters.
- A team is positioned well if the ball-carrying opponent can no longer play a

line ball and is prevented from dribbling by the double coverage (sideline + lateral and head-on opposition pressure).

- The advantage of this type of pressing is that the opponent is put under pressure on the sideline and is spatially restrained.

- In order to be able to exercise neat and effective pressing, strong communication between the players and scrupulous corrections from the coach are needed.

Field size:
Whole playing field

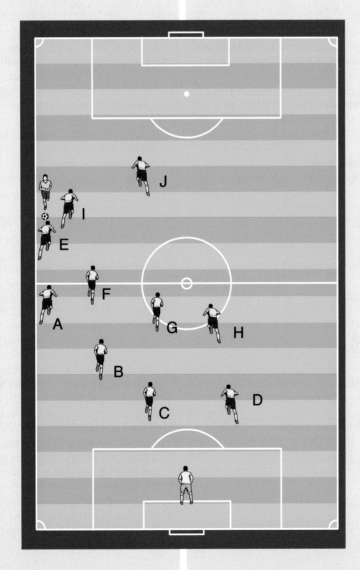

Training Target
- **Tactics**

Training Emphasis
- **Four man backfield**

Training Aspects

Training structure:	Progression, Main point/Emphasis
Duration:	1-10 min

Organization:

The team is positioned on the playing field in the defensive basic 4-4-2 formation in the defensive pressing zone. A player (or the coach) runs with the ball near the left-hand touchline towards the striker. The team shifts to the final position as shown in the picture. The positions can be doubly/multi occupied without problems.

Completing the drill:

In contrast to a central attacking player, the player coming down the flanks is marked by the striker closest to the ball (here J), who consequently impedes the path into the middle. The second striker (I) can either offensively press the ball-carrying player, i.e. block the path to the opposition goalkeeper/defenders, or safeguard the path to pass/run into their own half. The outer right midfielder H blocks the way down the sideline and prevents deep forward passes or runs. He double covers the ball-carrying player together with striker J. The defensive and midfield lines shift likewise as shown in the diagram towards the ball (in each case a crescent-shaped alignment of the two rows). If the final position has been achieved and the paths and distances are correct, the players go back to their starting positions and the drill starts anew.

Tips:

- The players located in a straight extension to the ball in den 4-4-2 formation (H and D) leave their linear formation most distinctly forward in comparison to the other players. This ensures that triangular coverage is formed and the direct path to goal is blocked at an early stage (shadow coverage). For better clarification, it may help to compare the ball to a magnet. The players who are positioned in front of the magnet are more strongly "attracted" to it than the others.
- This exercise is a dry run. There is no tackling. Its main function is the learning of paths used in soccer.
- The drill should be trained as many times as possible to ensure automatic movement sequences.
- The focus lies solely on the paths of the team. For example, when the play will be different if the attacking left-back's path is followed. The players should be aware that in a similar situation during a game they must be able to implement these paths without much time to think.
- The distance between each player varies depending on the speed of the play, changes in ball possession, etc. Players are usually 7 to 15 meters across and deep from each other.
- The distance in depth inside the triangles is 8-10 meters and 7-12 meters in width between the two players at the back.
- The team play on a field with dimensions of 30-35 x 30-35 meters.

- A team is positioned well if the ball-carrying opponent can no longer play a line ball and is prevented from dribbling due to double coverage (sideline + lateral and head-on opposition pressure).
- The advantage of this type of pressing is that the opponent is put under pressure on the sideline and is spatially restrained.

- In order to be able to exercise neat and effective pressing, strong communication between the players and scrupulous corrections from the coach are needed.

Field size:
Whole playing field

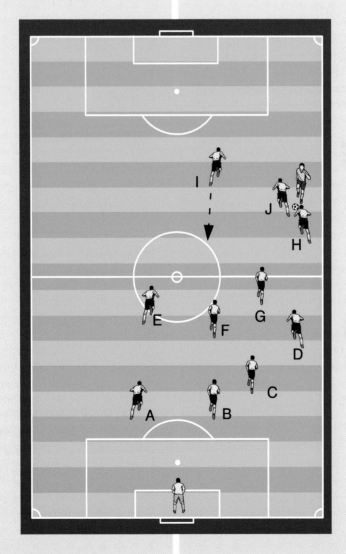

Training Target
- Tactics

Training Emphasis
- Four man backfield

Training Aspects

Training structure:	Progression, Main point/Emphasis
Duration:	1-10 min

Organization:
The team is positioned on the playing field in the defensive basic 4-4-2 formation in the defensive pressing zone. The team shifts to the final position as shown in the picture. A ball acts as the point of orientation for the players (they will press the ball). The positions can be multi-occupied without any problems.

Completing the drill:
In the depicted example, the ball is located in the inside left midfielder F's ball zone. At the signal of the coach, the team presses the ball. In doing so, player F and striker I double cover the ball, in each case head-on. The two other midfielders near the ball, G and H, position themselves behind F (shadow coverage) and the striker J either blocks the route behind (in the direction of the opponent's goal) or positions himself to form a triangle with G and H so that the path for a pass behind the two midfielders closes. The defensive and midfield lines shift likewise according to the diagram towards the ball (in each case there's a crescent-shaped alignment of the two rows). When the final position has been achieved and the paths and distances are correct, the players go back to their starting positions and the exercise starts anew.

Tips:
- The players located in a straight extension to the ball in the 4-4-2 formation (F, B) leave their linear formation most disinctly forward in comparison to the other players. This ensures that triangular coverage is formed and the direct path to goal is blocked at an early stage (shadow coverage). For better clarification, it may help to compare the ball to a magnet. The players who are positioned in front of the magnet are more strongly "attracted" to it than the others.
- This exercise is a dry run. There is no tackling. Its main function is the learning of paths used in soccer.
- The drill should be trained as many times as possible to ensure automatic movement sequences.
- The focus lies solely on the paths of the team. For example, when the play will be different if the inner left midfielder's path is followed. The players should be aware that in a similar situation during a game they must be able to implement these paths without much time to think.
- The distance between each player varies depending on the speed of the play, changes in ball possession, etc. Players are usually 7 to 15 meters across and deep from each other.
- The distance in depth inside the triangles is 8-10 meters and 7-12 meters in width between the two players at the back.
- The team play on a field with dimensions of 30-35 x 30-35 meters.
- A team is positioned well if the ball-carrying opponent can no longer play a

ball forward and is prevented from dribbling by double coverage.

- In order to be able to exercise neat and effective pressing, strong communication between the players and scrupulous corrections from the coach are needed.

Field size:
Whole playing field

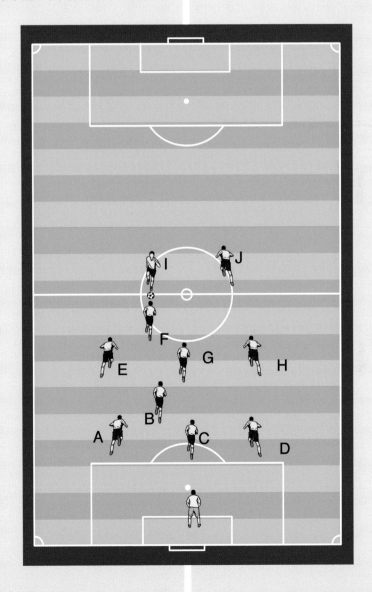

Training Target
- Tactics

Training Emphasis
- Four man backfield

Training Aspects

Training structure:	Progression, Main point/Emphasis
Duration:	1-10 min

Organization:

The team is positioned on the playing field in the defensive basic 4-4-2 formation in the defensive pressing zone. The team shifts to the final position as shown in the picture. The ball acts as the point of orientation for the players (they will press the ball). The positions can be doubly/multi-occupied without any problems

Completing the drill:

In the depicted example, the ball is located in the inside right midfielder G's ball zone. Upon the signal of the coach, the team presses the ball. In doing so, player G and striker J double cover the ball, in each case head-on. The two other midfielders near the ball, F and H, position themselves behind G (shadow coverage) and the striker I either blocks the route behind (towards the opponent's goal) or positions himself to form a triangle with F and E so that the path for a pass behind the two midfielders closes. The defensive and midfield lines shift likewise according to the diagram towards the ball (in each case there's a crescent-shaped alignment of the two rows). When the final position has been achieved and the paths and distances are correct, the players go back to their starting positions and the exercise starts anew.

Tips:

- The players located in a straight extension to the ball in the 4-4-2 formation (G. C) leave their linear formation most distinctly forward in comparison to the other players. This ensures that triangular coverage is formed and the direct path to goal is blocked at an early stage (shadow coverage). For better clarification, it may help to compare the ball to a magnet. The players who are positioned in front of the magnet are more strongly "attracted" to it than the others.
- This exercise is a dry run. There is no tackling. Its main function is the learning of paths in soccer.
- The drill should be trained as many times as possible to ensure automatic movement sequences.
- The focus lies solely on the paths of the team. For example, whn the play will be different it the inner right midfielder's path is followed. The players should be aware that in a similar situation during a game they must be able to implement these paths without needing much time to react.
- The distance between each player varies depending on the speed of the play, changes in ball possession, etc. Players are usually 7 to 15 meters across and deep from each other.
- The distance in depth inside the triangles is 8-10 meters and 7-12 meters in width between the two players at the back.
- The team play on a field with dimensions of 30-35 x 30-35 meters.

- A team is positioned well if the ball-carrying opponent can no longer play a ball forward and is prevented from dribbling by double coverage.
- In order to be able to exercise neat and effective pressing, strong communication between the players and scrupulous corrections from the coach are needed.

Field size:
Whole playing field

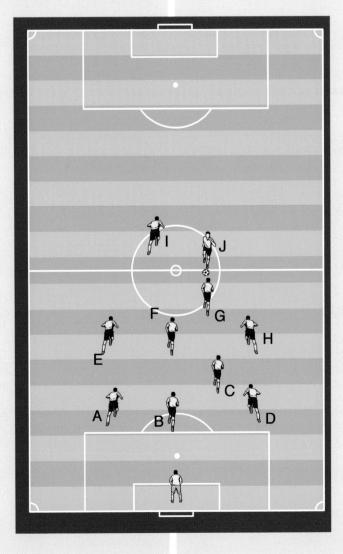

Training Target
- Tactics

Training Emphasis
- Four man backfield

Training Aspects

Training structure:	Progression, Main point/Emphasis
Duration:	1-10 min

Organization:
The team is positioned on the playing field in the defensive basic 4-4-2 formation in the defensive pressing zone. The team shifts to the final position as shown in the picture. The ball acts as the point of orientation for the players (they will press the ball). The positions can be multi-occupied without any problems.

Completing the drill:
The ball is located in the defensive zone between the outer left midfielder E and the left back A. Both of the players shift forward towards the ball. Player E presses from the side, A head-on from behind and player F blocks the way for a diagonal through ball. The strikers lurk behind the ball. Striker I moves towards the ball while Striker J moves more towards the opponent's back area. The defensive and midfield lines shift likewise according to the diagram towards the ball (in each case there's a crescent-shaped alignment of the two rows). When the final position has been achieved and the paths and distances are correct, the players go back to their starting positions and the exercise starts anew.

Equipment:
1 goal.

Tips:
- The players located in a straight extension to the ball in the 4-4-2 formation (A, E) leave their linear formation most distinctly forward in comparison to the other players. This ensures that triangular coverage is formed and the direct path to goal is blocked at an early stage (shadow coverage). For better clarification, it may help to compare the ball to a magnet. The players who are positioned in front of the magnet are more strongly "attracted" to it than the others.
- This exercise is a dry run. There is no tackling. Its main function is the learning of paths in soccer.
- The drill should be trained as many times as possible to ensure automatic movement sequences.
- The focus lies solely on the paths of the team. For example, when the play will be different if the outer left midfielder's and the left back's path is followed. The players should be aware that in a similar situation during a game they must be able to implement these paths without having much time to think.
- The distance between each player varies depending on the speed of the play, changes in ball possession, etc. Players are usually 7 to 15 meters across and deep from each other.
- The distance in depth inside the triangles is 8-10 meters and 7-12 meters in width between the two players at the back.
- The team trains on a field with dimensions of 30-35 x 30-35 meters.

- A team is positioned well if the ball-carrying opponent can no longer play a ball forwards and he is prevented from dribbling by double coverage.
- In order to be able to exercise neat and effective pressing, strong communication between the players and scrupulous corrections from the coach are needed.

Field size:
Whole playing field

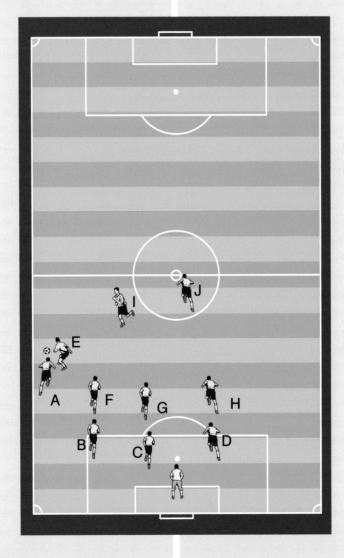

Training Target
- **Tactics**

Training Emphasis
- **Four man backfield**

Training Aspects

Training structure:	Progression, Main point/Emphasis
Duration:	1-10 min

Organization:
The team is positioned on the playing field in the defensive basic 4-4-2 formation in the defensive pressing zone. The team shifts to the final position as shown in the picture. The ball acts as the point of orientation for the players (they will press the ball). The positions can be multi-occupied without any problems

Completing the drill:
The ball is located in the defensive zone between the outer right midfielder H and the right back D. Both of the players shift forwards towards the ball. Player H presses from the side, D head-on from behind and player G blocks the way for a diagonal through ball. The strikers lurk behind the ball. Striker J moves towards the ball while Striker I moves more towards the opponent's back area. The defensive and midfield lines shift likewise according to the diagram towards the ball (in each case there's a crescent-shaped alignment of the two rows). When the final position has been achieved and the paths and distances are correct, the players go back to their starting positions and the exercise starts anew.

Equipment:
1 goal.

Tips:
- The players located in a straight extension to the ball in the 4-4-2 formation (G, D) leave their linear formation most distinctly forward in comparison to the other players. This ensures that triangular coverage is formed and the direct path to goal is blocked at an early stage (shadow coverage). For better clarification, it may help to compare the ball to a magnet. The players who are positioned in front of the magnet are more strongly "attracted" to it than the others.
- This exercise is a dry run. There is no tackling. Its main function is the learning of paths used in soccer.
- The drill should be trained as many times as possible to ensure automatic movement sequences.
- The focus lies solely on the paths of the team. For example, when the play will be different if the outer right midfielder's and the righ back's path is followed. The players should be aware that in a similar situation during a game they must be able to implement these paths without much time to think.
- The distance between each player varies depending on the speed of the play, changes in ball possession, etc. Players are usually 7 to 15 meters across and deep from each other.
- The distance in depth inside the triangles is 8-10 meters and 7-12 meters in width between the two players at the back.

- The team trains on a field with dimensions of 30-35 x 30-35 meters.
- A team is positioned well if the ball-carrying opponent can no longer play a ball forwards and he is prevented from dribbling by double coverage.

- In order to be able to exercise neat and effective pressing, strong communication between the players and scrupulous corrections from the coach are needed.

Field size:
Whole playing field

Training Target
- Tactics

Training Emphasis
- Four man backfield

Training Aspects

Training structure:	Progression, Main point/Emphasis
Duration:	1-10 min

Organization:
The team is positioned on the playing field in the defensive basic 4-4-2 formation in the defensive pressing zone. The team shifts to the final position as shown in the picture. The positions can be multi-occupied without problems. The ball acts as the point of orientation for the players (they will press the ball).

Completing the drill:
The ball marks the place where the opponent's left striker played to. Because the ball is located in a central position on the field, the ball is approached from two sides head-on. In this case, the players are the right side central defender C and the inner right midfielder G. Both players move to the ball in a way that stops a pass or moves forward or backward. The players F and H move slightly back and block the right and left through ball path. The two defenders B and D likewise move slightly back and move inward to form a triangle with C. The strikers lurk in the center circle. The defensive and midfield rows likewise shift (as shown on the diagram) towards the ball where in multiple triangle formations are thus created. When the final position has been achieved and the paths and distances are correct, the players go back to their starting positions and the exercise starts anew.

Tips:
- The players located in a straight extension to the ball in the 4-4-2 formation (C, G) leave their linear formation most distinctly forward in comparison to the other players. This ensures that triangular coverage is formed and the direct path to goal is blocked at an early stage (shadow coverage). For better clarification, it may help to compare the ball to a magnet. The players who are positioned in front of the magnet are more strongly "attracted" to it than the others.
- This exercise is a dry run. There is no tackling. Its main function is the learning of paths used in soccer.
- The drill should be trained as many times as possible to ensure automatic movement sequences.
- The focus lies solely on the paths of the team. For example, when the play will be different if the opponent's attacker's path is followed. The players should be aware that in a similar situation during a game they must be able to implement these paths without much time to think.
- The distance between each player varies depending on the speed of the play, changes in ball possession, etc. Players are usually 7 to 15 meters across and deep from each other.
- The distance in depth inside the triangles is 8-10 meters and 7-12 meters in width between the two players at the back.
- The team acts on a field with dimensions of 30-35 x 30-35 meters.
- A team is positioned well if the ball-carrying opponent can no longer play a

ball forwards and he is prevented from dribbling by double coverage.

- In order to be able to exercise neat and effective pressing, strong communication between the players and scrupulous corrections from the coach are needed.

Field size:
Whole playing field

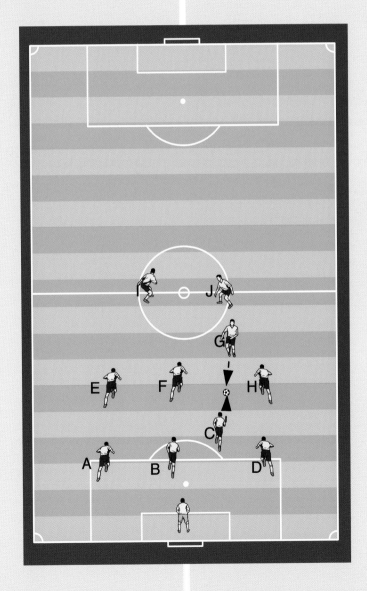

Training Target
- Tactics

Training Emphasis
- Four man backfield

Training Aspects

Training structure:	Progression, Main point/Emphasis
Duration:	1-10 min

Organization:
One team (yellow) is positioned on the playing field in the defensive basic 4-4-2 formation in the defensive pressing zone. This team shits into the final position shown in the diagram. The positions can be multi-occupied without problems. A second team (blue) is likewise aligned into 4-4-2 in offensive formation (the two wingbacks and the two outer midfielders move forwards). The blue team has possession of the ball.

Completing the drill:
One of the two blue central defenders starts off with a pass between the defending team's two rows of four. The yellow team's defensive and midfield rows move so that both of the defensive midfielders drop from mid-range into a deeper position where they have the opponents in front of them and the inner left midfielder F can attack the blue player receiving the pass. The central defender B may have to intervene and challenge head-on/double cover the receiver of the pass. This means that the right side central defender C has to move to the left and that player D must move in slightly without letting his man out of his sight. When the final position has been achieved and the paths and distances are correct, the players go back to their starting positions and the exercise starts anew.

Tips:
- Important is the formation of defensive triangles, double covering the receiver of the pass with the corresponding moving in of the right-sided central defender and the right back, as well as the offset in depth from the two midfielders E and G, who must slump back behind the line in level with the ball.
- This exercise is a dry run. There is no tackling. Its main function is the learning of paths used in soccer.
- The drill should be trained as many times as possible to ensure automatic movement sequences.
- The focus lies solely on the paths of the team using the example of a pass between the two lines of four. The players should be aware that in a similar situation during a game they must be able to implement these paths without much time to think.
- The distance between each player varies depending on the speed of the play, changes in ball possession, etc. Players are usually 7 to other.
- The distance in depth inside the triangles is 8-10 meters and 7-12 meters in width between the two players at the back.
- The team trains on a field with dimensions of 30-35 x 30-35 meters.
- A team is positioned well if the ball-carrying opponent can no longer play a ball forward and he is prevented from dribbling by double coverage.
- In order to be able to exercise neat and effective pressing, strong communication

between the players and scrupulous
corrections from the coach are needed.

Training Target
- **Tactics**

Training Emphasis
- **Four man backfield**

Training Aspects

Training structure:	Progression, Main point/Emphasis
Duration:	1-10 min

Organization:

The three yellow players B, C and D stand in their positions in the basic back four (aligned) formation at the beginning. The blue player E has the ball and takes it to the position shown in the diagram on the right-hand touchline. The left back A stands diagonally across from E. The players follow the paths marked in the picture during the course of the drill. The positions of the yellow players B, C and D can be multi-occupied without any problems.

Completing the drill:

The left back A is outplayed by E near the goal and there is no possibility for him to attack player E. Now the left side central defender B orientates himself outwards and puts player E under pressure. Player A takes the position of player B in the back four as quickly as possible (i.e., he replaces and safeguards B). The players C and D likewise move in and safeguard. After every move, the players take up their original positions and the drill starts anew.

Tips:

- This exercise is a dry run. There is no tackling. Its main function is the learning of paths used in soccer.
- The drill should be trained as many times as possible to ensure automatic movement sequences.
- The lateral distance between the players is 7-12 meters.
- The players are encouraged to communicate with each other and mutually direct each other. The coach must pay scrupulous attention adherence to the paths.

Field size:
Whole playing field

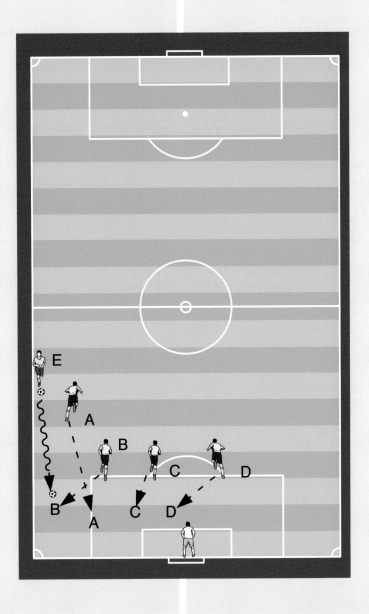

Training Target
- **Tactics**

Training Emphasis
- **Four man backfield**

Training Aspects

Training structure:	**Main point/Emphasis**
Duration:	**1-10 min**

Organization:
The three yellow players B, C and D stand in their positions in the basic back four (aligned) formation at the beginning. The blue player E has the ball and takes it to the position shown in the diagram on the right-hand touchline. The left back A stands diagonally across from E. The players follow the paths marked in the picture during the course of the drill. The positions of the yellow players B, C and D can be multi-occupied without any problems.

Completing the drill:
The blue player E starts a dribble along the sideline. Player A takes up the chase and attempts to catch up with him. Due to the possibility that player A may catch up with him, the row of three shifts only slightly to the left and moves laterally backwards. In this situation, their focus lies on safeguarding the potential goal scoring area. If it is apparent at an early stage that A can no longer apprehend player E, player B should attempt to attack player E as far away from goal as possible, and C and D should move to protect the goal. After every move the players take up their original positions and the drill starts anew.

Equipment:
1 goal.

Tips:
- This exercise is a dry run. There is no tackling. Its main function is the learning of paths used in soccer.
- The drill should be trained as many times as possible to ensure automatic movement sequences.
- The lateral distance between the players is 7-12 meters.
- The three defenders don't all shift to an even level, but stand staggered so that B is the deepest positioned player and C and D in each case are offset further forward.
- The players are encouraged to communicate with each other and mutually direct each other. The coach must pay scrupulous attention to the paths.

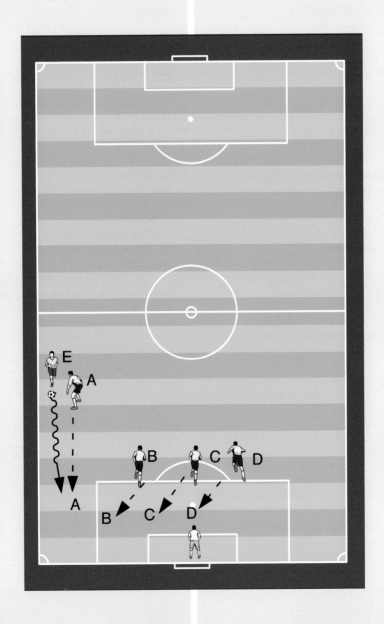

Training Target
- **Tactics**

Training Emphasis
- **Four man backfield**

Training Aspects

Training structure:	Progression, Main point/Emphasis
Duration:	1-10 min

Organization:
The team is positioned on the field in the basic formation of the 4-4-2 formation in the midfield pressing zone. The two blue players K and L, of whom K has the ball, position themselves on the playing field in accordance with the diagram. The team shifts in the paths shown in the diagram during the course of the drill. The positions of the team can be multi-occupied without any problems.

Completing the drill:
The player K has the ball and is pressed by the yellow team. Now he hits a long line ball to player L at the back of the moved up defense. The yellow team must now switch quickly and deprive player L of a shot on goal. As the left back has pushed up too far in order to close L, the left side central defender B assigns himself the ball-carrying L. The right side central defender C moves in and safeguards, just as the right back D does. The outer right midfielder H moves into the back four and thus becomes the right back. The left back A sprints at the highest speed to L in order to double cover him together with B. When the sequence has been completed and the paths, as well as the distances of the players to each other, are correct, the players go back to their starting positions and the exercise starts anew.

Tips:
- The taking over of the wingback position by player B and the dropping back of the outer right midfielder into the right back position is vital in this drill; as is the energetic and prompt pursuit by A.
- The midfielders also orientate themselves backwards.
- This exercise is a dry run. There is no tackling. Its main function is the learning of paths used in soccer.
- The drill should be trained as many times as possible to ensure automatic movement sequences.
- The focus lies solely on the paths of the team using the example of a long line pass in the back of the two lines of four. The players should be aware that in a similar situation during a game they must be able to implement these paths without much time to think.
- The distance between each player varies depending on the speed of the play, changes in ball possession, etc. Players are usually 7 to 15 meters across and deep from each other.
- The studying of the paths in the team unit requires intensive communication within the team and scrupulous corrections by the coach

Training Target
- **Tactics**

Training Emphasis
- **Four man backfield**

Training Aspects

Training structure:	Progression, Main point/Emphasis
Duration:	1-10 min

Organization:
The set up of a back four in linear formation (blue players) and positioning of a team (yellow) in the offensive basic formation of the 4-42 system in the attacking pressing zone. This team moves into the final position shown in the picture. The positions can be multi-occupied without any problems. The right side central defender (K) has the ball.

Completing the drill:
The team pushes out of the basic formation to player K as follows: The left striker I pushes head-on from the front to K, the striker J closes the diagonal passing route in the center. The inner left midfielder F and the left side central defender B move forward out of their positions and form triangles with the players next to them (E and G, as well as A and C) to prevent passes (shadow coverage). The rest of the players move in the direction of the ball and hence make the area tight and put the opponent under pressure. When the final positions have been achieved and the paths and distances are correct, the players go back to their starting positions and the exercise starts anew.

Tips:
- It is important that the team move in a body forwards and as a group prevent player K from structurally building up play.
- This exercise is a dry run. There is no tackling. Its main function is the learning of paths used in soccer.
- The drill should be trained as many times as possible to ensure automatic movement sequences.
- The focus lies solely on the paths of the team. For example, when the play will be different if the right-sided central defender of the opposition team's path is followed. The players should be aware that in a similar situation during a game they must be able to implement these paths without having much time to think.
- The distance between each player varies depending on the speed of the play, changes in ball possession, etc. Players are usually 7 to 15 meters across and other.
- The distance in depth inside the triangles is 8-10 meters and 7-12 meters in width between the two players at the back.
- The team trains on a field with dimensions of 30-35 x 30-35 meters.
- A team is positioned well if the ball-carrying opponent can no longer play a ball forwards and he is prevented from dribbling by double coverage.
- In order to be able to exercise neat and effective pressing, strong communication among the players and scrupulous corrections from the coach are needed.

When completing the drill, there are four zones, in which the opponent can be pressed. They are:

- Attacking pressing zone
- Midfield pressing zone
- Defensive pressing zone
- Stand deep/dropping pressing zone

In the beginning one should learn the basic rules of pressing and zone play and then subsequently learn the exceptions. It is important to differentiate between a passive defense and an active defense. In a passive defense, the purpose is to keep the opponent away from goal through clever movement. One way this happens is when the opponent must play the ball back or generally doesn't get to attempt a shot on goal. This occurs frequently without winning possession. When actively pressing, the purpose is to attain possession of the ball. Ultimately, pressing means building a trap for the opponent. Pressure is built for as long as it takes for the opponent to make a mistake and for access to the ball to be made possible. If the player expecting or occupying possession of the ball is not open (e.g., with his back to the defender) then the possibility of accessing the ball is at its most promising.

If play is channeled out or the central defender is run at as when

- Shifting together – right/left central defender opens up play
- Shifting together – possession with right back/left back

then one assumes a more passive and hard-running pressing. For the strikers, this means covering longer paths in order to arrive in the double covering position.

In the examples
- 4-4-2 in linear formation in order to channel the play inward
- 4-4-2 with diamond in order to channel the play inward

one assumes, in contrast, a more active pressing, as the paths here are shorter.

Pressing the flanks is more suited to keeping the opponent away from goal. Pressing inside serves more to coming into possession when in larger numbers. Good communication and observation is important for this. It is vital here to anticipate and attempt to take possession at the right moment. The player is always in a good position to take possession when he is an arm's length away from the opponent. The strikers take up an important role in pressing. Ultimately they decide how and when to run or in which direction to channel. A striker always runs diagonally to the defender and not in an arc-shaped path. The defenders have the most passive part to begin with in well-functioning pressing.

The following terminology is used in defensive work/pressing:

Channel/run at: The player decides how he must run at the player in possession of the ball so that he has to pass.

Shift: The players move according to the path of the ball, moving in its direction and taking up their corresponding positions.

Indenting: According to the position of the ball, the players safeguard through a path going deeper.

Building pressure: Pressure on the opponent is built through the distance to the ball-carrying player and the channeling of the game until taking regaining possession or until the teammates and opponent have been brought into the ideal position.

Apprehending: The distance between the player in possession and the defending player should be at the most an arm's length. The challenging player attempts to come into possession or force his opponent into passing.

Double covering: Two players attack the player expecting or occupying the ball at the same.

Breaking off: A player, mostly a central defender, is encouraged to drop deep in order to prevent a pass behind the line. This prevents playing for offside.

Securing: A teammate protects the challenging player from behind.

Offside: The player in possession of the ball is attacked so that the player who is located at the back is untended, meaning a pass to him would generate an offside position.

Moving out: When the team is standing deep or the distances between the individual parts of the team are too big, a directive will be issued to move out or to reduce the distance from the next part of the team.

Communication: The players should talk with each other and mutually support each other.

Ultimately it is the coach who decides which plan or alternative the team is to press/defend.

Training Target
- Tactics

Training Emphasis
- Four man backfield

Training Aspects

Training structure:	Main point/Emphasis
Duration:	10-30 min

Organization:

Setup of a back four in linear formation plus a midfielder (blue player). The opposing team (yellow) is in the offensive basic formation of the 4-4-2 in the midfield pressing zone. The yellow team moves into the final position shown in the picture. The positions can be multi-occupied without any problems. The blue team's right side central defender (K) has the ball.

Completing the drill:

The passing sequence occurs when striker I runs to central defender K, K passes to L, and L, after being run at by E, passes to midfielder M. The defending team moves out of the basic formation toward player K as follows: The left striker I channels the play through a diagonal run from the front, somewhat laterally offset from K, so that he can no longer pass to the left side central defender. The striker J runs diagonally in the direction of the opposing midfielder M in order to double cover him with midfielder F. F is positioned so that the ball-carrier M cannot turn out, but has to turn in to striker J who then has access to the ball, or vice versa (that he must turn to F). The inner right midfielder G and the left side central defender B move diagonally forward out of their positions and form triangles with the players next to them to prevent passes (shadow coverage). When the final positions have been achieved and the paths and distances are correct, the players go back to their starting positions and the exercise starts anew.

The aim is to channel the opening up of play by the opponents so that they must pass inward and possession can be captured by outnumbering the opponent, which should lead to a quick counterattack toward goal. If such a capture of possession succeeds 4-7 times per half of the game, then the team will have an outstanding starting position to score goals. However, it is advisable to play the ball in the direction of the goal (and not away from the goal), which requires that the strikers start on a purposeful path towards the goal.

Tips:
- It is important that the team moves as a unit forward and, as a group, prevents players K, L and M from structurally building up play.
- This exercise is a dry run. There is no tackling. Its main function is the learning of a basic soccer play.
- The drill should be trained as many times as possible to ensure auomatic movement sequences.
- The focus lies solely on the paths of the team. For example, when the play will be different if the right-sided central defender of the opposition team's path is followed. The players should be aware that in a similar situation during a game they must be able to implement these paths without much time to think.
- The distance between each player varies depending on the speed of the play, changes in ball possession, etc. Players are usually 7 to 15 meters across and deep from each other.

- The distance in depth inside the triangles is 8-10 meters and 7-12 meters in width between the two players at the back.
- The team trains on a field with dimensions of 30-35 x 30-35 meters.
- A team is positioned well if the ball-carrying opponent can no longer play a ball forwards and he is prevented from dribbling by double coverage.

- In order to be able to exercise neat and effective pressing, strong communication among the players and scrupulous corrections from the coach are needed.

Field size:
Whole playing field

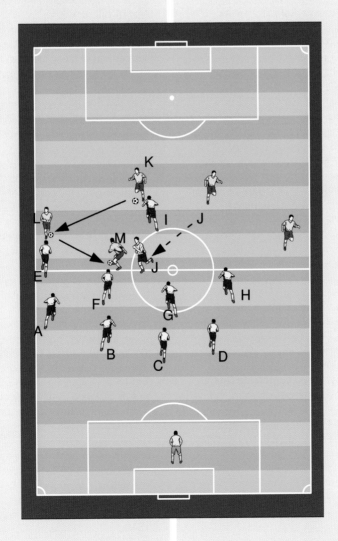

Training Target
- **Tactics**

Training Emphasis
- **Four man backfield**

Training Aspects

	Main point/Emphasis
Training structure:	
Duration:	10-30 min

Organization:
Setup of a back four in linear formation plus a four man midfield (blue player). The opposing team (yellow) in the offensive diamond formation of the 4-4-2 in the midfield pressing zone. The yellow team moves into the final position shown in the picture. The positions can be multi-occupied without any problems. The blue team's right sided central defender (K) has the ball.

Completing the drill:
The team moves out of the basic positions as follows: Strikers I and J position themselves in the direction of the sidelines in order to prevent a pass to the wingbacks. Therefore they attempt to tempt the central defender K into a dribble through the middle with a consequential pass to player L. The inner left midfielder E can laterally double cover the ball carrying L with midfielder G, or midfielder F can double cover L head-on with G, and so have superior numbers and obtain the ball. The rest of the players move in the direction of the ball and therefore restrict the space and put their opponents under pressure. When the final positions have been achieved and the paths and distances are correct, the players go back to their starting positions and the exercise starts anew.
The aim is to channel the play to the center in order to outnumber and put pressure on the player in possession thereby obtaining possession of the ball from them.

Tips:
- It is important that the team moves as a unit forward and, as a group, tempts player K into a dribble or pass through the middle.
- This exercise is a dry run. There is no tackling. Its main function is the learning of paths used in soccer.
- The drill should be trained as many times as possible to ensure automatic movement sequences.
- The focus lies solely on the paths of the team. For example, when the play will be different if the central midfielder of the opposition team's path is followed. The players should be aware that in a similar situation during a game they must be able to implement these paths without much time to think.
- The distance between each player varies depending on the speed of the play, changes in ball possession, etc. Players are usually 7 to 15 meters across and deep from each other.
- The distance in depth inside the triangles is 8-10 meters and 7-12 meters in width between the two players at the back.
- The team trains on a field with dimensions of 30-35 x 30-35 meters.
- A team is positioned well if the ball-carrying opponent can no longer play a ball forwards and he is prevented from dribbling or passing by double coverage.
- In order to be able to exercise neat and effective pressing, strong communication among the players and scrupulous corrections from the coach are needed.

Field size:
Whole playing field

Methodical set up of the 4-4-2 formation or the back four

1. Tactical meeting using flipchart, laptop and projector or by video presentation (before and after).
2. Position-based description of tasks on the tactics board.
3. Implementation of what has been learned in training exercises.

Training unit 4-4-2

Tactical movement in the 4-4-2 formation **123**
- Warming up in the 4-4-2 linear system .... .124
- Warming up in the 4-4-2 linear system with balls .... .126
- Warming up in the 4-4-2 diamond system with balls .... .128
- Alternative warming up routine – Running in chaines .... .130

Main part I **133**
- One attacker against two defenders .... .134
- Two against two with moving in .... .136
- Two defenders against three attackers .... .138
- Three defenders against five attackers .... .140

Main part II **142**
- Type of play I – path of the back-four with 8 players .... .142
- Type of play II – paths of the back four with 4 players + 1 .... .144
- Type of play III – 4 defenders against 7 attackers .... .146

Main part III **150**
- 4 defenders + 1 central midfielder against 7 attackers .... .150

End of Training **153**
- Another training example: 5 against 3 constantly in turns .... .154

Training Target
- **Tactics**

Training Emphasis
- **Positional Play**

Training Aspects

Skills involved:	Defensive play, Quick anticipation, Speed of movement off the ball, Quick decisions, Quick processing, Quickness of reaction, Pushing, Quick understanding of danger
Age level:	13-14 years, 15 years to Adult, Under 12, Under 13
Level of play:	Advanced
Type of training:	Team training
Training structure:	Warm-up, Progression
Purpose:	Defensive behaviors, Cooperation within the team, Improve individual qualities
Total number of players:	11 players or more
Participating players:	Whole team
Training location:	Asphalt, Turf field, Grass field
Dealing with space:	Limited playing field
Duration:	10-30 min
Physiology:	Soccer-specific endurance
Goal keeping:	1 goalie or more

Organization:
The team is positioned on the field in the defensive basic 4-4-2 formation in the defensive pressing zone.

Completing the drill:
All of the paths presented in the previous examples are studied together in the linear system. This involves the isolated paths in the back four defensive line, as well as all of the visualized team paths and options. The coach simulates the paths in the individual zones (e.g., offensive pressing, midfield pressing, pressing the left back, etc.) through using calls. The goalkeepers can occasionally participate with the outfield players in order to get a feel for the outfield players' tasks.

When the players have achieved their final positions, they stay where they are and the coach corrects any errors. Then they move on to the next training task.

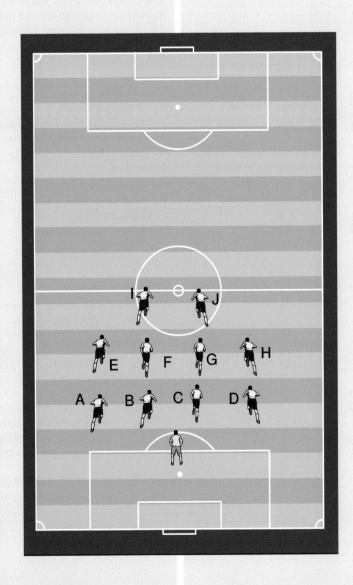

Training Target
- Tactics

Training Emphasis
- Positional Play

Training Aspects

Skills involved:	Defensive play, Quick anticipation, Quick decisions, Quick processing, Quickness of reaction, Pushing, Quick understanding of danger
Age level:	13-14 years, 15 years to Adult, Under 12, Under 13
Level of play:	Advanced
Type of training:	Team training
Training structure:	Warm-up, Progression
Purpose:	Defensive behaviors, Groups, Cooperation within the team, Improve individual qualities
Total number of players:	11 players or more
Participating players:	Whole team
Training location:	Asphalt, Turf field, Grass field
Dealing with space:	Limited playing field
Duration:	10-30 min
Physiology:	Soccer-specific endurance
Goal keeping:	1 goalie or more

Organization:
The team is positioned on the field in the defensive 4-4-2 basic formation in the defensive pressing zone.

Set up different colored zone cones on the sideline as shown in the diagram:

Red cone – defensive pressing zone
Blue cone – midfield pressing zone
Yellow cone – offensive pressing zone/fore checking

On the field, ten balls or cones are distributed (see diagram for positioning).

Completing the drill:
Implement the paths as in the previous practice, however this time balls (or cones) are distributed throughout the field. Each is assigned a number. Following the call of a number from the coach, the team moves to the corresponding ball or cone. When they have arrived in the final position the players remain where they are and the coach corrects any errors. The procedure is then continued (call a number, move).

Equipment:
1 goal

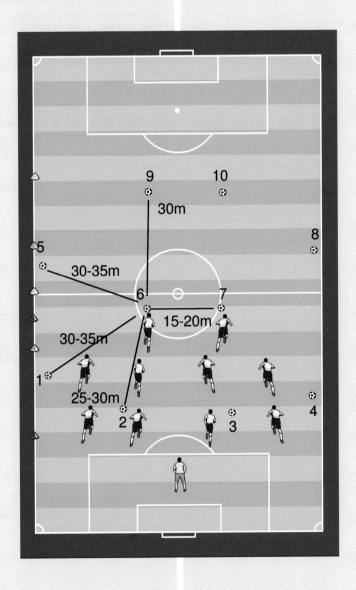

Training Target
- Tactics

Training Emphasis
- Positional Play

Training Aspects

Skills involved:	Defensive play, Quick anticipation, Quick decisions, Quick processing, Quickness of reaction, Pushing, Quick understanding of danger
Age level:	13-14 years, 15 years to Adult, Under 12, Under 13
Level of play:	Advanced
Type of training:	Team training
Training structure:	Warm-up, Progression
Purpose:	Defensive behaviors, Groups, Cooperation within the team, Improve individual qualities
Total number of players:	11 players or more
Participating players:	Whole team
Training location:	Asphalt, Turf field, Grass field
Dealing with space:	Limited playing field
Duration:	10-30 min
Physiology:	Soccer-specific endurance
Goal keeping:	1 goalie or more

Organization:
The team is positioned on the field in the defensive 4-4-2 basic formation in the defensive pressing zone. Set up of ten balls (cones) as shown in the diagram. The pressing zones can also be shown through different colored cones on the sideline (see the exercise: Warming up in the 4-4-2 linear system with balls).

Completing the drill:
Set up of the ball/cone orientated paths in the diamond formation over the whole field. The balls are assigned numbers. When the coach calls out a number, the players run to the corresponding ball or cone in a team-tactical pressing group. From the diamond formation, a line of three with an attacking midfielder in front comes about in the defensive group. The players in front move in the spaces between the corresponding midfielders or close the space in the middle when the ball comes.

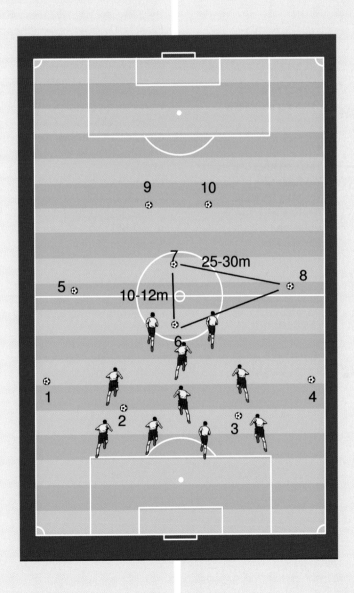

Training Target
- Tactics

Training Emphasis
- Positional Play

Training Aspects

Skills involved:	Defensive play, Quick anticipation, Speed of movement off the ball, Quick decisions, Quick processing,, Quickness of reaction, Pushing, Quick understanding of danger
Age level:	13-14 years, 15 years to Adult, Under 12, Under 13
Level of play:	Recreational
Type of training:	Team training
Training structure:	Warm-up, Progression
Purpose:	Defensive behaviors, Training for fun Groups, Part of a team, Cooperation within the team, Improve individual qualities
Total number of players:	10 players
Participating players:	Whole team
Training location:	Asphalt, Turf field, Grass field
Dealing with space:	Limited playing field
Duration:	10-20 min
Physiology:	Soccer-specific endurance

Organization:

The players are bound to each other by a rope (7-15 meters) apart and run in 4-4-2 lines.

Set up different colored zone cones on the sideline as shown in the diagram:

Red cone – defensive pressing zone
Blue cone – midfield pressing zone
Yellow cone – offensive pressing zone/fore checking

On the field, ten balls or cones are distributed (see diagram for positioning).

Completing the drill:

The coach assigns the balls (cones) numbers. When the coach calls a number, the player must move to the corresponding ball (cone). When they have reached their final positions there, they stand still and the coach corrects any errors. The coach can also call out a pressing zone (e.g., offensive pressing). In this situation, the players move together into the corresponding position.

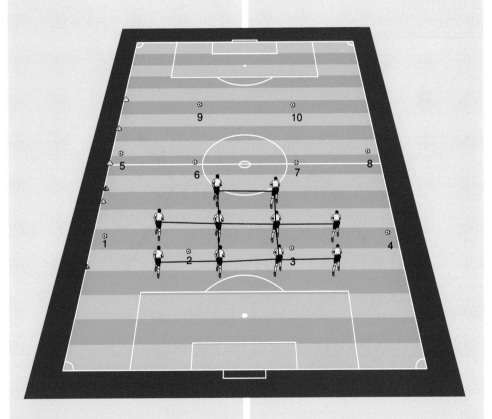

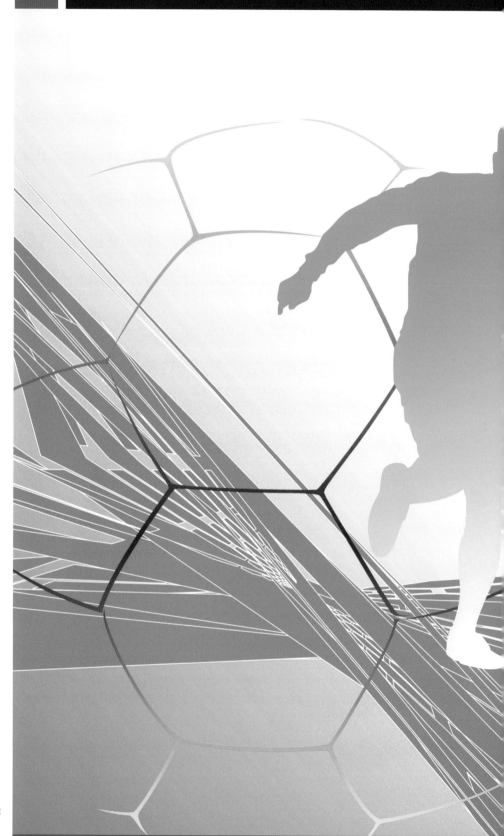

Main part

Main part I **134**

Main part II **142**

Main part III **150**

Organization:
- 1 attacker against 2 defenders with shuttling, safeguarding and moving in.
- 2 on 2.
- 2 defenders against 3 attackers with shifting and moving in.
- 3 defenders against 5 attackers, the defenders play in a line of three, the attackers in a 3-2-formation (2 strikers, 1 central midfielder and 2 outer midfielders).

All sequences of play are played with a full-sized goal with goalkeeper.

Training Target
- Tactics

Training Emphasis
- Four man backfield

Training Aspects

Skills involved:	One on one, Leaping strength, Defensive/Offensive play, Speed of movement with ball, Attacking down the middle, Quick anticipation, Outside of the foot, Control, Trapping into space, Speed of movement off the ball, Dribbling, Quick decisions, Quick processing, Inside of the foot, Inside of the laces passing, Combining technical skill with movement, Body fake, Running technique with/without ball, Quickness of reaction, Speed in change of direction, Man down/Man up, Pushing Laces,, Quick understanding of danger, Taking on multiple players
Age level:	13-14 years, 15 years to Adult, Under 12, Under 13
Level of play:	Recreational
Type of training:	Group training
Training structure:	Progression, Main point/Emphasis
Purpose:	Defensive behaviors, Offensive behaviors, Improve individual qualities
Total number of players:	4 or more players
Participating players:	Whole team
Training location:	Any
Dealing with space:	Half-field
Duration:	10-20 min
Physiology:	Soccer-specific endurance, Power & Speed
Goal keeping:	1 goalie

Organization:

A goalkeeper and three outfield players are positioned on the field as shown in the diagram. The two blue players act as defenders, the red player as an attacker. The attacker has the ball.

Completing the drill:

The goalkeeper opens the play with a pass/throw to the attacker C waiting on the halfway line.
The ball-carrying attacker runs to the defender B. In doing so he dribbles, feinting to the left and right. Player A safeguards player B by mirroring the changes of direction that C makes.

If player B is outplayed, defender A apprehends player C immediately and B safeguards player A from behind as soon as possible and follows the lateral changes in direction of player A. The attacker attempts to out-dribble the two defenders and get a shot on goal through fast dribbling. Depending on the situation, he may use feints/dummies.

Equipment:
1 full size goal

Field size:
30 x 40 m

Tips:
- At the beginning, the striker should run to the defenders at only a moderate speed in order to give them as good a chance as possible to tailor their paths to each other.
- The distance of the defender behind to the one in front should always be about 5 meters.
- If the first defender is outplayed, the defender behind runs to the attacker. When he is about 2-3 meters in front of him he reduces his speed, comes to a standstill and running diagonally backwards, takes up the speed of the attacker.

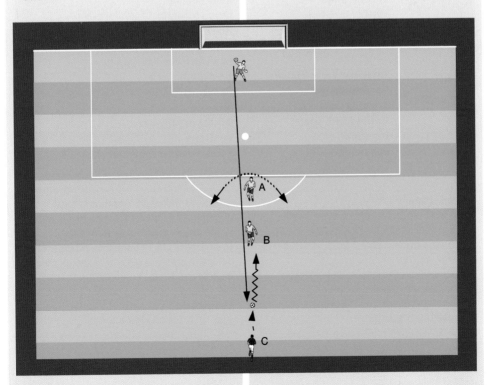

Training Target
- **Tactics**

Training Emphasis
- **Four man backfield**

Training Aspects

Skills involved:	One on one, Leaping strength, Defensive/Offensive play, Speed of movement with ball, Quick anticipation, Outside of the foot, Controlling the ball, Control, Speed of movement off the ball, Wall passes, Quick decisions, Running off the ball, Quick processing, Overlapping, Inside of the foot, Inside of the foot passing, Inside of the laces passing, Combining technical skill with movement, Short passing, Running technique with/without ball, Quickness of reaction, Speed in change of direction, Man down/Man up, Pushing, Volley, Laces, Quick understanding of danger, Advanced passing
Age level:	15 years to adult
Level of play:	Recreational
Type of training:	Group training
Training structure:	Main point/Emphasis
Purpose:	Defensive behaviors, Offensive behaviors, Improve individual qualities
Total number of players:	5 players or more
Participating players:	Whole team
Training location:	Any
Dealing with space:	Double penalty box
Duration:	15-30 min
Physiology:	Soccer-specific endurance, Power & Speed
Goal keeping:	1 goalie

Organization:
Five players position themselves on the playing field as shown in the diagram. The two blue players A and B are the defenders; the two red players are the attackers. The goalkeeper goes in goal. The ball is with red player C in the starting position.

Completing the drill:
Player C starts play with a pass to D. As soon as C moves to strike the ball, defender B runs to/attacks player D. When player B

leaves his defensive position in the direction of D, player A takes up his position in the defense. Now a 2 on 2 situation with continuously changing paths occurs until the defender wins possession or the attacker makes an attempt on goal.

Equipment:
1 full-size goal, 6 cones

Tips:

- This pattern of play's main function is for the learning of paths used in soccer. The tackling carried out, however, is fully active and with full physical exertion.
- The drill should be trained as many times as possible to ensure automatic movement combinations.
- Attention should be paid to a precise and punchy passing/attacking game.
- The start signal for the counterreaction is the passer of the ball moving to strike the ball. The lateral distances between the players are 7-12m. The playing partners stand at a distance of about 15m opposite from each other.
- If one of the defenders safeguards the other from behind, he should move 5m diagonally behind the man in front.

Field size:
Double the 18-yard box

Distances between the cones:
Width: 32 m
Length: 16 m

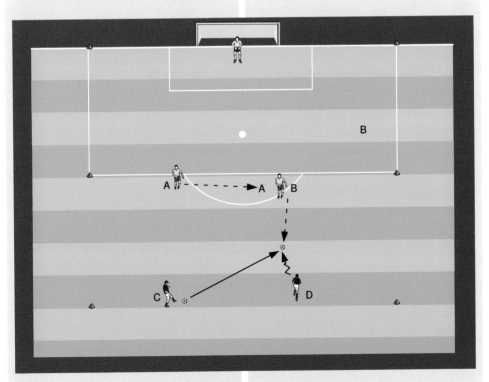

Training Target
- Tactics

Training Emphasis
- Four man backfield

Training Aspects

Skills involved:	One on one, Leaping strength, Defensive/Offensive play, Speed of movement with ball, Quick anticipation, Outside of the foot, Controlling the ball, Quick decisions, Quick processing, Overlapping, Inside the foot, Inside of the foot passing, Inside of the laces passing, Combining technical skill with movement, Heading while in motion, Body fake, Passing over multiple stations, Quickness of reaction, Speed in change of direction, Pushing, Volley, Laces, Quick understanding of danger, Taking on multiple players, Advanced passing
Age level:	13-14 years, 15 years to Adult, Under 12, Under 13
Level of play:	Recreational
Type of training:	Group training
Training structure:	Main point/Emphasis
Purpose:	Defensive behaviors, Offensive behaviors, Improve individual qualities
Total number of players:	6 or more players
Participating players:	Whole team
Training location:	Any
Dealing with space:	Limited playing field
Duration:	10-25 min
Physiology:	Soccer-specific endurance, Power & Speed
Goal keeping:	1 goalie

Organization:
A goalkeeper, two defenders (blue) and three attackers (red) are positioned, as shown in the diagram, on the playing field marked out by cones. The attackers have the ball.

Completing the drill:
The attackers attempt to outplay the defenders and attempt a goal through the use of different means of attack, such as quick passing combinations, overlapping, crossing over, through balls, dribbles and one-twos. The two defenders have to prevent this through clever tactical movement and aggressive conduct in the challenge. The offside rule applies.

Equipment:
1 full-size goal, 5 cones

Tips:
- The two defenders always act together and must not move too far away from each other.
- The aim is either to win possession of the ball or to force the attacker with the ball into a potential goal scoring area to the side and block the way for a pass toward the goal or a teammate by double covering him.

Field size:
50 x 40 m

Distances between the cones:
10 m

Training Target
- **Tactics**

Training Emphasis
- **Four man backfield**

Training Aspects

Skills involved:	One on one, Leaping strength, Defensive/Offensive play, Speed of movement with ball, Quick anticipation, Outside of the foot, Controlling the ball, Quick decisions, Quick processing, Overlapping, Inside of the foot, Inside of the foot passing, Inside the laces passing, Combining technical skill with movement, Heading while in motion, Body fake, Passing over multiple stations, Quickness of reaction, Speed in change of direction, Pushing, Volley, Laces, Quick understanding of danger, Taking on multiple players, Advanced passing
Age level:	13-14 years, 15 years to Adult, Under 12, Under 13
Level of play:	Recreational
Type of training:	Group training
Training structure:	Main point/Emphasis
Purpose:	Defensive behaviors, Offensive behaviors, Improve individual qualities
Total number of players:	9 players or more
Participating players:	Whole team
Training location:	Any
Dealing with space:	Limited playing field
Duration:	10-25 min
Physiology:	Soccer-specific endurance, Power & Speed
Goal keeping:	1 goalie

Organization:
A goalkeeper, three defenders (red) and five attackers (blue) are positioned, as shown in the diagram, on the playing field marked out by cones. The attackers have the ball.

Completing the drill:
The attackers attempt to outplay the defenders and attempt a goal through different means of attack, such as quick passing combinations, overlapping, crossing over, through balls, dribbles and one-twos. The three defenders have to prevent this through clever tactical movement and aggressive conduct in the challenge. The offside rule applies.

Equipment:
1 full-size goal, 5 cones

Tips:
- The defenders always act together and must not move too far away from each other.
- The aim is either to win possession of the ball or to force the attacker with the ball into a potential goal scoring area to the side and block the way for a pass toward the goal or a teammate by double covering him.
- The task of the defender nearest the ball is to press the ball-carrying player. The two other defensive players protect the area at the back (defensive triangle).

Field size:
50 x 40 m

Distances between the cones:
10 m

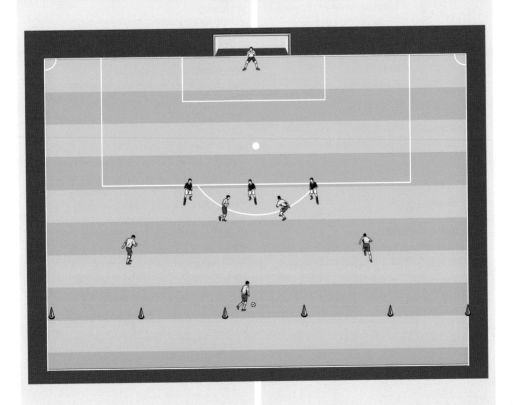

Training Target
- Tactics

Training Emphasis
- Four man backfield

Training Aspects

Skills involved:	Leaping strength, Defensive play, Speed of movement with ball, Quick anticipation, Trapping, Trapping into space, Quick decisions, Quick processing, Inside of the foot passing, Combining technical skill with movement, Short passing, Positional passing, Quickness of reaction, Opening the field in the four man backfield, Pushing, Quick understanding of danger
Age level:	13-14 years, 15 years to Adult, Under 12, Under 13
Level of play:	Advanced
Type of training:	Group training, Team training
Training structure:	Main point/Emphasis
Purpose:	Defensive behaviors, Improve individual qualities
Total number of players:	8 players
Participating players:	Defenders, Whole team, Midfielders
Training location:	Asphalt, Turf field, Grass field
Dealing with space:	Half-field
Duration:	10-20 min
Physiology:	Soccer-specific endurance, Power & Speed

Organization:
Eight players position themselves in two rows (four players per row) as shown in the diagram in one half of the field. Cones can be used to mark the playing positions. Player E has the ball.

Completing the drill:
Player E starts with a pass to player A. He runs to meet the ball, stops it halfway and stays still. The other players in the blue line of four shift or move in, just as the shifting of the line of four was studied in the previous exercises (also see the red path in the diagram). Players B, C and D thereby move sideways to the right in order to protect the deep area.

Subsequently A passes the ball back to E and A goes back to the basic formation. Player E plays the ball sideways to player F. He passes to player B who comes to the ball. Now the same running and passing sequence as before begins. Players A and C move 2-3 meters inward and protect B (forming triangles). D moves in to the right. When all 11 paths have been completed, the assignment of tasks is exchanged.
Now the blue players pass the ball and the red players practice the shifting/paths of the back four.

Equipment:
8 cones

Tips:
- The paths of the players are: to the ball and back as well as moving to the left and right.
- Often players move inward in a forward motion. Staggered depth should, however, be obtained and consequently the player must laterally move backwards.
- First practice the paths slowly. Later practice at a higher speed. Then the passing ensues.
- Speak with each other.
- Neat, accurate passing game.

Field size:
36 x 30 m

Distances between the cones:
Length: 30 m
Width: 10-12 m

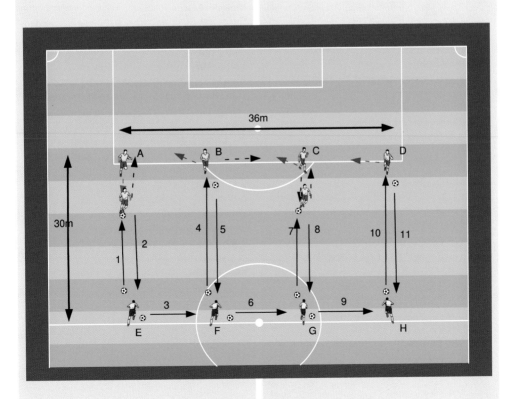

Training Target
- Tactics

Training Emphasis
- Four man backfield

Training Aspects

Skills involved:	Defensive play, Speed of movement with ball, Quick anticipation, Trapping, Quick decisions, Quick processing, Combining technical skill with movement, Short passing, Quickness of reaction, Pushing, Quick understanding of danger
Age level:	13-14 years, 15 years to Adult, Under 13, Under 12
Level of play:	Advanced
Type of training:	Group training, Team training
Training structure:	Warm-up, Progression
Purpose:	Defensive behaviors, Groups, Part of a team
Total number of players:	4 or more players
Participating players:	Defenders, Whole team, Midfielders
Training location:	Asphalt, Turf field, Grass field
Dealing with space:	Half field
Duration:	10-15 min
Physiology:	Soccer-specific endurance, Power & Speed

Organization:
Four players are positioned in linear formation even with the edge of the penalty area. The placement of cones can be used as distance markers. The passer of the ball positions himself in the center circle with the ball.

Completing the drill:
Player E passes the ball in the space in front of the back four (see the arrows). The back four move in the direction of the ball. The defender closest to the ball thereby moves out of the linear formation and attempts to reach the ball at the earliest possible moment and stop it. In the example of player C, the paths are obvious: Player C runs to meet the ball, stops it and stays where he is.
The other players in the blue back four now shift or move in as shown by the marked paths. Players A and B thereby move 2-3 meters sideways to the left and accordingly D moves 2-3 meters to the right in order to safeguard player C (forming triangles).
Player C then passes the ball back to E and the players go back to their basic positions. Then player E passes the ball on to player D, who runs to the ball and players A, B and C move 2-3 meters to the left in order to protect D.
When all four running and passing routes have been completed, the exercise starts anew.

Equipment:
4 cones

Tips:
- The paths of the players are: to the ball and back, as well as moving to the left and right.
- Often players move inward in a forward motion. Staggered depth should, however, be obtained and consequently the player must diagonally backwards.
- First practice the paths slowly. Later practice at a higher speed. Then the passing ensues.
- Speak with each other.
- Neat, accurate passing game.

Field size:
36 x 30 m

Distances between the cones:
Width: 10-12 m

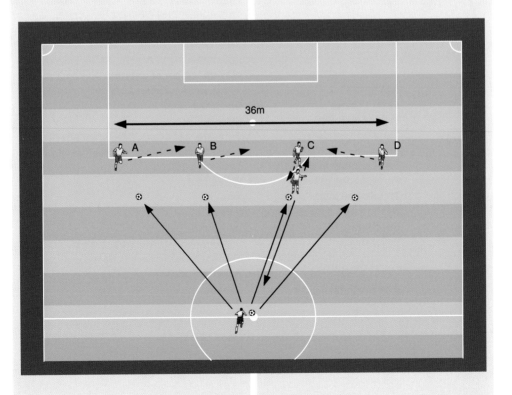

Training Target

- Tactics

Training Emphasis

- **High pressure on defense**
- **Quick transitioning (defense to offense)**
- **Countering**
- **Opening the field**
- **Four man backfield**

Training Aspects

Skills involved:	One on one, Leaping strength, Defensive/Offensive play, Speed of movement with ball, Attacking with focus on offsides, Offensive play, Attacking down the middle, Quick anticipation, Controlling the ball, Wall passes, Dribbling, Quick decisions, Wing play with opponents, Running off the ball, Quick processing, Overlapping, Inside of the foot passing, Combining technical skill with movement, Heading while in motion, Short passing, Body fake, Long passing, Passing in a triangle, Passing over multiple stations, Positional passing, Quickness of reaction, Transitional play (shifting the game), Offensive play with variable options, Man down/Man up, Pushing, Volley, Laces, Quick understanding of danger, Taking on multiple players, Advanced passing
Age level:	13 - 14 years, 15 years to Adult
Level of play:	Advanced
Type of training:	Group training
Training structure:	Defensive behaviors, Offensive behaviors,
Purpose:	Stress training, Improve individual qualities
Total number of players:	12 or more players
Participating players:	Whole team
Training location:	Any
Dealing with space:	Half-field
Duration:	20-40 min
Physiology:	Soccer-specific endurance, Training of elementary endurance II, Speed endurance, Power & Speed
Goal keeping:	1 goalie

Organization:

On the halfway line, three goals made from cones are placed. Two teams are formed: an attacking team with seven players (yellow) and a defending team (blue) with four players, which start in a back four linear formation (the basis formation). The yellow team deploys itself as shown in the diagram with a central point guard, two players in the midfield halfback positions, two wingers and two strikers. The yellow team has the ball. A goalkeeper is located in the goal.

Completing the drill:

The yellow team's task is to attempt a goal through the use of different moves and attacking variations. The blue team defends the big goal and has the possibility to score in the three cone goals when they have possession of the ball. When defending, it is imperative to shift correctly and not allow the other team any passing or shooting options. It is important that when the defender near the ball moves out, his two neighbors move in and build a defensive triangle.

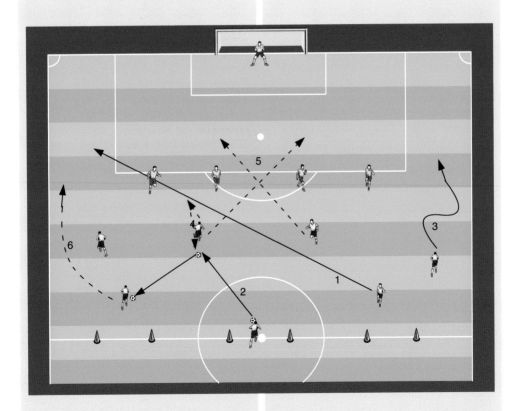

If the yellow team scores or if the ball goes behind the goal-line or sideline, the players start anew from the halfway line.

Zig-zag balls should start play. That means the strikers move in a counter movement and always offer themselves to the passer of the ball as a play to point in the middle of the field. Make as little ball contact as possible. On the sidelines, 1 on 1 and overlapping should be played when possible. In addition to this, the flank players must be positioned on the sideline and after a pass dribble inwards so that the wingback is able to overlap him. Always play diagonal balls and initiate changeovers so that the defensive unit is brought into action. The strikers always approach the player in possession, dart sideways and then cross over.

1. Diagonal ball
2. Zigzag ball
3. Dribble 1 on 1
4. Dart sideways
5. Cross over
6. Overlap

Equipment:
1 full-size goal, 6 cones

Tips:
- Through deep passes the defensive line is brought into forward motion. Through further shifting of the ball, the defensive line is forced to shift forward to the side. As a result, the attacking team obtains room in the deep areas, as well as the possibility to pass to the freed-up side through a diagonal pass.
- The players passing the ball into the area at the back must not run too close to the people in front of them and should keep a distance of 20-25 meters between themselves and the attackers so that the events in play are always in front of them and the balls can "run-in" so that with quick contact the ball can be passed on.
- Constant movement, talking with each other, and a quick, precise passing game are important.
- The back four must not forget the depth offset and must not let themselves be dragged too far out.

Field size:
Half a playing field

Distance between the cones:
3 m

Exclusive:

Since you have purchased this book, you have access to all exercises in digital format on: www.easy2coach.net

In order to visualize all the 4-4-2 systems, free animations are available.

www.easy2coach.net

How does it work:

1. Register for free at
   www.easy2coach.net/en/motions
2. Enter your voucher-code:
   MM2010E2Co2DS
3. Get unlimited access to all animations in this book

Training Target
- Tactics

Training Emphasis
- **High pressure on defense**
- **Quick transitioning (defense to offense)**
- **Countering**
- **Quick transitioning (offense to defense)**
- **Tacticall drills**
- **Positional Play**
- **Four man backfield**

Training Aspects

Skills involved:	One on one, Leaping strength, Defensive/Offensive play, Speed of movement with ball, Attacking with focus on offsides, Attacking down the middle, Quick anticipation, Controlling the ball, Dribbling, Quick decisions, Wing play with opponents, Running off the ball, Quick processing, Overlapping, Inside of the foot passing, Inside of the laces passing, Combining technical skill with movement, Heading while in motion, Body fake, Passing over multiple stations, Positional passing, Quickness of reaction, Direct play to the forwards, Building an attack over the wings, Man down/Man up, Pushing, Quick understanding of danger, Taking on multiple players
Age level:	13 - 14 years, 15 years to Adult
Level of play:	Advanced
Type of training:	Group training
Training structure:	Main point/Emphasis
Purpose:	Defensive behaviors, Offensive behaviors, Stress training, Improve individual qualities
Total number of players:	13 or more players
Participating players:	Whole team
Training location:	Asphalt, Turf field, Grass field
Dealing with space:	Half field
Duration:	20-40 min
Physiology:	Soccer-specific endurance, Power & Speed
Goal keeping:	2 goalies

Organization:

5 against 7 play in half of a field toward two goals. For this purpose a second goal is placed on the halfway line. The blue team is positioned in the back four basis formation with a central player in front of the line of four. The yellow team deploy themselves, as shown in the diagram, with a central point guard, two players in the midfield halfback positions, two wingers and two strikers. There is a goalkeeper in both goals. The balls are located in the yellow team's goal.

Completing the drill:

The yellow team's task is to have an attempt on goal through the use of different moves and attacking variations, and to protect their own goal when there is a counter from the yellow team. The blue team defends their goal and has the opportunity to score a goal themselves when they have possession. When defending, it is vital to shift correctly and not allow the opponent any options to pass or shoot on goal. It is important that when the defender near the ball moves out, his two neighbors move in and build a defensive triangle.

If the yellow team scores or if the ball goes behind the goal line or sideline the players start anew from the halfway line.

Zig-zag balls should start play. That means the strikers move in a counter movement and always offer themselves to the passer of the ball as a play to point in the middle of the field. Make as little ball contact as possible. On the sidelines 1 on 1 and overlapping should be played when possible. In addition to this, the flank players must be positioned on the sideline and after a pass dribble inwards so that the wingback is able to overlap him. Always play diagonal balls and in doing so initiate changeovers so that the defensive unit is brought into action. The strikers always approach the player in possession, dart sideways and then cross over.

Equipment:

2 full-size goals

Tips:

- Through deep passes, the defensive line is brought into a forward motion. Through further shifting of the ball, the defensive line is forced to shift forward to the side. As a result, the attacking team obtains room in the deep areas, as well as the possibility to pass to the freed-up side through a diagonal pass.
- The players passing the ball into the area at the back must not run too close to the people in front of them and should keep a distance of 20-25 meters between themselves and the attackers so that the events in play are always in front of them and the balls can "run-in" so that with quick contact the ball can be passed on.
- Constant movement, talking with each other, and a quick, precise passing game are important.
- The back four must not forget the depth offset and not let themselves be dragged too far out.

Field size:
Half a playing field

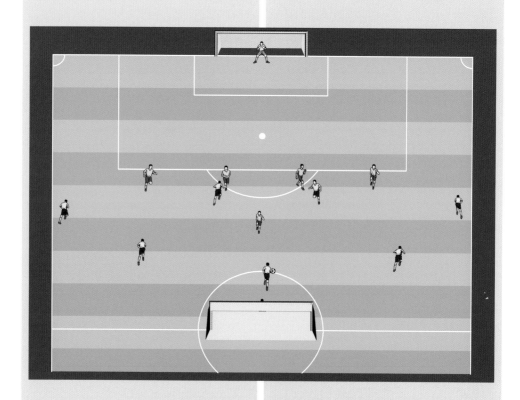

Training Target
- **Tactics**

Training Emphasis
- **Four man backfield**

Training Aspects

Age level:	13 - 14 years, 15 years to Adult
Level of play:	Recreational
Type of training:	Group training
Training structure:	Conclusion, End
Participating players:	Whole team
Training location:	Any
Dealing with space:	Free space
Duration:	5-10 min
Physiology:	Regeneration

Completing the drill:
Warm down and stretch.

Training Target
- Tactics

Training Emphasis
- Four man backfield
- Quick transitioning (defense to offense)
- Countering
- Positional play

Training Aspects

Skills involved:	One on one, Leaping strength, Defensive/Offensive play, Speed of movement with ball, Quick anticipation, Controlling the ball, Dribbling, Quick decisions, Wing play with opponents, Overlapping, Inside of the foot passing, Inside of the laces passing, Combining technical skill with movement, Heading while in motion, Body fake, Passing over multiple stations, Quickness of reaction, Man down/Man up, Pushing
Age level:	13-14 years, 15 - 16 years, Under 12, Under 13
Level of play:	Advanced
Type of training:	Group training, Team training
Training structure:	Main point/Emphasis
Purpose:	Defensive behaviors, Offensive behaviors, Improve individual qualities
Total number of players:	17
Participating players:	Whole team
Training location:	Asphalt, Turf field, Grass field
Dealing with space:	Half field
Duration:	25-40 min
Physiology:	Soccer-specific endurance, Training of elementary endurance II, Power & Speed
Goal keeping:	2 goalies

Organization:
Three teams of five are formed. On the halfway line, 5 against 3 is played with two goals. A second goal is placed on the halfway line. When two of the three teams are playing against each other, the third team stands behind the attacking team's goal. The balls are shared between the two goals.

Completing the drill:
Team A begins with all 5 players against 3 players from team B (the two missing players from B have a break level with the halfway line and to the side of the playing field or as shown in the diagram next to the side of the goal. They take part in the game as soon as their team goes into attack). After the end of the attack, or if team B dribbles the ball over the halfway line after winning possession, all 5 players from team B play against 3 defenders from team B. The teams rotate constantly in this order. The defensive line is a back three and the attackers should play in a 1-2-2 formation when possible.

Equipment:
2 full-size goals, 2 cones

Tips:

- The focus of this sequence of play is on the quick switch from defense to attack and the training of outnumbered/outnumbering plays.
- When attacking, constant movement, talking with each other, and a quick and precise passing game are necessary. Hence, in accordance with 1-2-2 formation, a depth offset from the players must be guaranteed and consequently movement in line is avoided.
- The defenders always move together and must not move too far away from each other.
- The defenders' aim is either to win possession or to force the ball-carrying attackers in potential goal-scoring areas out to the side, and by double covering

him, preventing a pass path toward the goal or his teammate.

- The task of the defender close to the ball is to press the ball-carrying player. The two other defensive players protect the space behind (defensive triangle).

Field size:
Half a playing field

Distances between the cones:
45-70 m (depending on the width of the field)

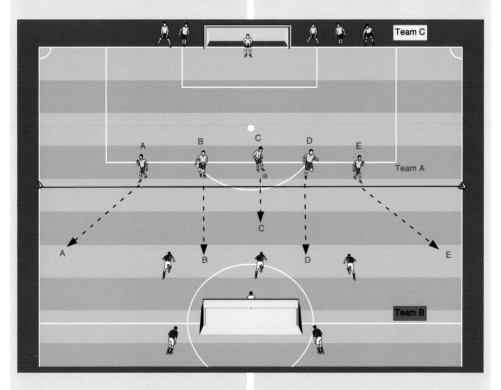

Many years ago the desire grew in me to put on paper and possibly publish all the knowledge and experience I gathered, first as a player and coach and later on during the internships, the coaching seminars and during the countless conversations with soccer enthusiasts. This book and the many others made it all come true.

I want to thank the following people and businesses:

Easy2Coach, who have given me new ways of showing the countless exercises graphically with their drawing software Easy2Coach Draw.

Together with the Meyer and Meyer publishing house I was able to publish my ideas world-wide and on various types of media (books, eBooks, numerous training packages as well as exercises in an online data base with integrated drawing and animation software).

Günter Limbach for his faith and his legal advice.

My father Johannes Titz, whom I could always count on, who has shown me my first steps in soccer and who never tired submitting more drawings of different exercises.

Meyer and Meyer publishing house and particularly Jürgen Meyer for the faith, the conviction and the helpful advice. Sebastian Stache, always by my side as a partner, a critic and a friend and who happens to be one of the best proofreaders any author could hope for.

My friend Prof. Dr. Steven Dooley who inspired me with his critical and constructive comments.

Thomas Dooley for his professional co-author ship and his faith in our coaching approach.

Timo Nagel, a friend and coaching colleague who stood by me for years with advice and support.

Finally I want to thank all the people who have supported me along this path and who have inspired my creativity. My family deserves the biggest thanks for taking the backseat all too often and for their relentless support throughout the entire process. Thank you!

Christian Titz